# A
# STRAIGHTFORWARD
# GUIDE
# TO
# TEACHING YOUR CHILD
# TO READ AND WRITE

VALERIE DOUGLAS
STRAIGHTFORWARD PUBLISHING

Straightforward Publishing
38 Cromwell Road
Walthamstow
London E17 9JN

© Valerie Douglas 1998

Second Edition 1998

**ISBN 1899924 97 3**

Cover design by Straightforward Graphics

Printed by BPC Information Ltd Exeter.

## ABOUT THE AUTHOR

Valerie Douglas has been a primary school teacher for over forty years and, for ten of these, a head teacher. She has had extensive experience of remedial teaching and, having taken early retirement from the state sector, now runs a very successful private remedial service giving individual tuition to pupils aged from five to fifty-five.

CONTENTS
**Introduction**

## 3 Methods of Teaching Reading 32

Shifts of Focus
The Alphabet Approach
The Phonic Approach
The Sentence Method
The Whole Word Method
Reading Programmes
Initial Teaching Alphabet
Individualised Reading
Developmental Learning
Key Points

## 4 Books 42

Choosing Books
Small Children
Pictures
Interactive Books
Repetition
Stories with a Moral/Story Tapes
Quality and Price
Parental Preferences
Reading Schemes
Real Books
Books Based on Everyday Experiences
Controlled Vocabulary Schemes
Libraries
Key Points

## 5 Starting School 49

Preparation
Playgroups and Nursery Schools

Explanations
The Modern Classroom
Parental and Teacher Concerns
Sharing Sessions
Name Cards
Projects
Computers
Judging Progress
Key Points

## 6  Beginning to Write  57

Complexities
The English Writing System
First Stages
Initial Enthusiasm/Incorrect Spelling
Learning to Spell
Spelling Schemes
Punctuation
Legible Handwriting
Speech Experiences and Creative Writing
Rough Drafts, Conferences and Final Copy
Key Points

## 7  Parental Support for Schools  64

Parental Attitude and School Success
Home/School Relations
Educational Aspects
Professional Aspects
Problems Arising from Parental Help
Political/Financial Aspects
How to Support
Key Points

## 8 When Things Go Wrong 71

Emotional Effects of Failure
Backwardness and Delinquency
The National Curriculum
Infant/Junior Schools
Physical Factors
Social Factors
Emotional Factors
General Intelligence
Specific Difficulties
Measuring Success
Parental Complaints
Parental Rights/Actions
Transfer
Private Tuition
Help from Parents
Affection and Support
Progress and Mistakes
Reading Readiness
Self-Reliance and Responsibility
Older Non-Readers
Using Established Interests
Formal Approach
A Basic Lesson
Key Points

## 9 Testing 86

Testing Your Own Child
Choosing the Time and Place/ Setting the Scene
Beginning the Tests
Reading Tests: Holborn Sentence Scale
Schonell Graded Word Reading Test
Spelling Test: Schonell Spelling Test

# TEACHING YOUR CHILD TO READ AND WRITE

## BY VALERIE DOUGLAS.

Target audience defined as:-

1)  Parents who want to 'do the right thing' from their child's babyhood, to ensure they develop literacy easily and efficiently.

2)  Parents who are concerned because their child cannot read and write by age seven +.

3)  Parents who are expected by schools to help their children with reading at home.

4)  Those who realise that current 'child centred' methods have failed and need information and guidance on how to use the more traditional methods of teaching reading and writing.

# INTRODUCTION.

In a world full of words, most parents want their children to learn to read and write quickly and efficiently. This book is intended for them. It is for parents who wish to ensure that their children, from babyhood, are on the right path to literacy and gives suggestions and ideas of how these early years can be used to prepare children for reading and writing.

So called 'trendy' methods, used in many schools today, have in fact delayed this process for a great many. Indeed, by the time they start Junior school, too high a proportion of children have barely begun to read and this is a cause of great concern for parents. This book aims to address their problems. Clearly and concisely it sets out and evaluates the main methods of teaching literacy and, drawing upon the author's forty-odd years of experience, suggests ways of developing an interest in and love of words.

Further, it is intended to help the numerous parents who are called upon by their children's schools to help with reading at home. With no experience of teaching and little help from the professionals this can be an onerous task. Many parents have no idea of what is expected of them, even of how to begin, and the nightly ritual of the school reading book becomes a nightmare for parent and child. This book is intended to help and advise them, to give them confidence to accept the task gladly.

This was not written as a book for professionals (although with the government's call for a return to more traditional methods, some might find Chapter Three helpful).Primarily it gives straightforward, simple information and ideas, specifically for parents, grandparents, aunts and uncles or any layman who wants to help a child towards a love of books and competent literacy. Reading is fun. Writing is fun. Hopefully this book will help you to enjoy them with your children.

The second edition of this book contains an added chapter on assessing your child. Whilst there may be inherent difficulties in this for the layman, it is included in response to many requests from parents who need to know how their children are performing in relation to their peers.

A last point: Literacy is a gift for life. If you can help your child towards it you will be opening doors to a wider, more exciting and fulfilling future.

The book is arranged as follows:

**Chapter One** deals with the importance of early stimulation and the significance of spoken language and play. It suggests ways of involving your child from a very early age in activities which will lead to reading and writing readiness.

**Chapter Two** covers factors which lead to reading success.

**Chapter Three** describes and evaluates the various methods of teaching reading.

**Chapter Four** discusses reading books, their composition, print, illustrations, vocabulary and content.

**Chapter Five** is about starting school. It discusses how to prepare your child and describes the approach and set-up you are likely to encounter in the modern classroom.

**Chapter Six** deals with writing, how it develops, how it is likely to be approached in school.

**Chapter Seven** discusses parental support for schools and its underlying reasons. It suggests ways and means and gives a list of dos and don'ts.

**Chapter Eight** is concerned with what happens when things go wrong. It examines possible reasons, suggests how to consult with schools and gives a framework for remedial help at home.

**Chapter Nine** deals with testing. Reading and spelling tests are included, laterality is discussed and testing for mixed laterality is described.

**The Conclusion** draws together the threads of the previous chapters into an overview of literacy and its importance in the modern world.

Note: Throughout this book the child is referred to as 'he'. This denotes no sexism on the part of the author and is solely a matter of convenience and convention.

# 1

# EARLY YEARS

---

## STIMULATION

A child's first years are the most important in his whole life. Early childhood is a crucial period for mental growth and the most vital developments occur before schooling begins. At least 50% of a child's mental capacities have developed by the age of five and by then personality is largely fixed.

Individual characteristics affect a child physically, mentally, emotionally and in the speed and thoroughness of his learning. Children are entirely individual but all show the same pattern of development and all respond to stimulation. While the child's innate temperament will play a part in the development of his personality and intellect, the way people treat him at home and the experiences and opportunities offered him there are of inestimable importance. His learning depends upon them. Children need a continuous relationship with a caring, interested adult within an exciting, stimulating environment during these formative years if they are to develop their full potential and take easily to literacy.

Even before they are born babies react to the stimulus of sound and soon after birth respond to a known voice. Their eyes follow a bright light and the softest touch on a baby's cheek will cause him to turn his head towards it. The new born's senses are already highly developed and the more they are stimulated the more discriminating and accurate they become. Parents know instinctively how to talk and sing to their babies, stroke and caress them, make silly noises, wave rattles before them, hang coloured mobiles over their cots and generally bombard their senses from all directions -

and babies thrive on it. From their very earliest days they are social beings and need social contact. Babies who are ignored and isolated fail to thrive as they should.

Nevertheless, babies also need quiet time on their own, time to amuse themselves, kicking and babbling, watching the world around them. Shops are full of toys suitable for these times - musical mobiles, cradle toys, activity centres, baby gyms - but putting the pram under a line pegged with brightly coloured towels or ribbon streamers blowing in the wind or positioning it so that the baby can look through branches and leaves to the sky can be just as entertaining. So, too, can watching the laundry go round and round in the washing machine or the vacuum cleaner scudding across the floor. This may all seem a far cry from reading and writing but, in fact, anything which interests a baby, makes him curious, persistent, puzzled, helps him develop the attitudes and skills which have a very definite bearing on the growth of literacy.

## SPOKEN LANGUAGE

As they learn to talk babies find themselves in the perfect learning situation. They are immersed in words, adults talk to them as if they could already understand and reinforce their babblings by showing utter delight at any near-recognisable words. The baby is rewarded immediately with attention, approval and affection. He is showered with extravagant praise and is encouraged to repeat his new word over and over again. This positive reinforcement is so effective that the baby persists and before long is using the most complicated language structures easily and effectively.

The importance of language development where literacy is concerned cannot be over stressed. First a child must assimilate and develop spoken language as a vehicle of communication and a means of expressing ideas, thoughts and emotions. This ability to learn language starts young and lessens as the child grows older so it is essential to encourage the development of language skills from a very early age. Children should have unlimited opportunities of talking freely with adults, having their questions answered, having things carefully explained.

Not only must parents talk with children, they must also provide experiences which give rise to natural and purposeful speech, encouraging them to put these experiences into words. Going through the car wash, riding on the top deck of a bus, a visit to the swimming pool, making cakes, dusting - these and similar activities taken in the company of a loved adult can lead to fluent, expressive speech and a torrent of questions needing answers.

Listening carefully to small children can be not only interesting and amusing but also a very rewarding experience. Within days they grasp some new language concept and use it correctly and the speed of their progress can be phenomenal. An ability to use the spoken word must precede reading and writing and a child must understand spoken sentences before he can take in printed ones.

Rhymes and jingles have a special fascination during these early years, presenting new speech patterns for children to try out again and again. Quite small babies enjoy "Round and round the garden", "This little piggy", "Pat a cake" with their mix of action and familiar words while older children not only learn rhymes and songs but often repeat them simply for their own pleasure.

**THE BEDTIME STORY**

Ours was an oral tradition and whilst now it is mostly embodied in print rather than passed on by word of mouth the bedtime story situation remains a significant part of it and is a particular, special delight for children. Moreover, reading regularly with your child, enjoying books together, has real value in promoting literacy. For the child it is an enriching experience, satisfying and meaningful. Sitting close to a loved adult, enjoying his or her complete attention, children are enthralled by the unfolding story, whether it is about the world they know or completely beyond it. They are gripped by the excitement of books and begin to understand what reading is all about. They perceive it as fascinating, something which reveals new ideas, which entertains and delights, something which adults do - powerful motives for wanting to read themselves. They become familiar with the special language of books, with the conventions of print and story telling. Gradually they realise that the lines and curves on the page tell them something they want to know, can provide pleasure and interest, hide a story within them.

## SHARING BOOKS

Start by sharing picture books , talking about the illustrations, pointing to things in the pictures and involving the child. "Where is the dog? Show me the baby. Can you find the mouse?" Then move to books with pictures and clear, bold print. Encourage the child to notice the difference between text and pictures. "Look. These marks tell me the words to say. This word is..." Show the direction of print by following the words with a finger as you read them. Draw attention to word spaces so that he begins to see words as separate units. Point out the difference between telling and reading a story. Ask questions about the book. Show just a picture and ask, "Can I read this page?" or one with words and pictures and ask, "What tells me the words to say?" Ask where the story begins and where it ends. Show the child how to open and hold a book correctly and to return it carefully when the story is finished. Even a small child should not be allowed to throw books down, tear or chew them, walk on or drive toys over them. Show your child that books should be treated with care, for the more they are respected the more magical they become. Make sure he understands the correct vocabulary;-look, listen, find, first, last, beginning, end, word, space, letter. Teach him as you go, "Look. That word says dog. Can you see it anywhere else on the page?"

## EMERGING LITERACY

While all this is going on you are easing your child towards a stage of emerging literacy when he will want to begin to read and write. Very soon you will find him showing reading- type behaviour, sitting quietly with a book, turning the pages and telling himself the story, emulating the adult's behaviour when reading to him. Of course he is not really reading yet but he is certainly making giant steps towards it. He knows what books are for, he knows he can gain pleasure and excitement from them, he knows how to handle them and he knows all about communicating through words, spoken and written. This behaviour arises quite spontaneously, without any adult direction and entirely for his own pleasure. Strategies of mature reading are being developed and the close visual and tactile contact with books will bear him in good stead later.

## PLAY

Once upon a time gives a wonderful  structure for play and through it a child can work out his fantasies and interpret his world. Even in these fairly enlightened days some adults think of play as a waste of time. The very opposite is true. Play provides a major means of learning and through it a child grows and develops.  He plays in ways which increase his skills, understanding or power and through play he adds to his knowledge of the world. He can be completely absorbed in solving a problem - fitting the pieces of a jigsaw together, finding a way to catch a bubble without bursting it - using persistence and concentration. Absorbtion in play is a healthy sign, an indication of mental health. Children who fail to play often fail at school. Those who play well tend to work well.

## PLAY MATERIALS

Good play materials need not be expensive and a little thought and ingenuity can provide hours of pleasure. We all know that the child would rather play with the box than the toy and a collection of large cardboard boxes is easily obtained and replaceable. Try to provide something for physical activities (climbing, swinging, jumping, riding), materials for making things (playdough, paint, paper, glue, scissors, fabric), and fantasy materials (dressing up clothes, prams, house toys, sand, water, painting, drawing, boards, chalks).

## SOLITARY/SOCIAL PLAY

Some play should be solitary and giving opportunities for playing alone (without a background of blaring music or television) is a good training for reading and writing which are both solitary activities. Children who have missed out on this experience often find it difficult to get on with work by themselves at school. Much play is social and it can be an enlightening experience to watch and listen to a group of children playing in the home corner, pretending to be the adults around them, getting an imaginative insight into the grown-ups attitudes, acting out their behaviour. Play activities can have a therapeutic effect and bring relief from pressure. A child can play out his worries and do things in "pretend" mode that he could not possibly do in reality. However, play can, also, develop key characteristics which are useful for later school success: concentration, persistence, problem solving, an enquiring mind, a lively imagination, self motivation and linguistic skills.

## GETTING STARTED WITH WORDS

A child who has had rich language experiences, is familiar with books, has enjoyed stories, rhymes and songs, has asked many questions and received answers, had extensive opportunities for play and lots of exciting experiences may well find learning to read an easy task. Some will start reading of their own accord as if by magic. For those who do not there is much that can be done to ease the process. Given that the child is ready to read (and little is achieved if he is not) you can begin by showing him what his name looks like when it is written. Do not make the mistake of writing it all in capitals. Point out that the first letter of a name is always a capital (or 'big letter') but the rest are lower case ('small letters').

## SIGHT WORDS

Many parents begin by teaching children their letters (i.e. the names and sounds of the alphabet) but this is rarely the best way to start. Leave it for later and begin by getting the child to recognise whole words, not just any old words but those which have special meaning for him. Start with his name. Write it on the pictures he draws or paints, cards he sends. Print it clearly on a piece of card (about 10" by 4") in thick, black, felt tip pen and give it to him. Very quickly he will come to recognise its characteristic shape. Prove this by writing several words on a piece of paper and ask if he can show you which one is his name. Once he has learnt its visual pattern he can start building up a set of sight words which are meaningful to him. I use bright orange card (8" by 3") and let the child choose his own words. (Recently an almost-three-year-old asked for 'chips', chocolate' and 'flowers' "because I like them". He learnt them instantly and three weeks later still recognises them.)

Point out words in the environment - Bus Stop, Push, Pull, Open, Closed, Fish and Chips, Newsagent etc. and put labels round the house - hot and cold on the taps, window, door, toy cupboard. Let the child suggest labels he would like (the same almost-three-year-old wanted 'Digger's Cottage' on the dog kennel) and change them frequently to keep up the interest. Collect the labels and let the child put them back in the right places. Every time he gets it right give extravagant praise, a hug and a kiss. If he gets it wrong avoid any hint of criticism or disapproval. Using intense positive reinforcement like this is wonderfully effective. The child feels good about himself. He is pleased and excited by his success and wants to learn more and more. Playing games with the cards adds variety. Make two of each and play Snap. Make some activity cards:

clap your hands

close your eyes

stand up

Hold up one of them and ask the child to do what it says. Make sentence cards, two copies of each, and cut one into separate words so that the child can match them to the whole sentence:

| 1 AM JAMES |
| --- |

| 1 | | AM | | JAMES |

remembering always that the more important the words are to the child the more likely he is to remember them.

## VISUAL PATTERNS

It is thought that children respond to the total visual pattern of a word initially and that the difference in the overall shapes of words helps him distinguish one from the other. Every word has a distinct visual pattern which is affected by the shape of the letters and its length. A child notices projecting letters especially and remembers

elephant     train     aeroplane

more easily than

was   saw   on   no

which are frequently confused

## INDIVIDUAL LETTERS

Recognising words is not dependent upon knowing the letters that make them up but at this stage you can begin pointing them out and saying their names and sounds. "Look. This letter with a stick going down and a round bit at the top is a letter p. We make the sound of this letter at the beginning of pig, p p p pig." Tell the child that letters can be written in two ways -'big' and 'small'. Be honest about the fact that a letter does not always make the same sound. "We say its sound l in lovely but l in milk."
A good way of familiarising small children with letters is to choose one every week and concentrate on it. You could cut out a large s in lint, dampen it, sprinkle cress seeds over it  and have a green, growing s within a few days. You could paint and draw "s" make a big one to go on the

22

wall, collect lots of things that begin with s and put them together on a table with a giant s hanging above it.

## SCRIBBLING/DRAWING

Reading and writing go hand in hand and while all this is going on children should be having plenty of opportunities to draw and scribble. They find wall boards and chalk wonderful. (Try putting a blackboard in the child's room or, better still, painting the lower half of a wall with blackboard paint.) Large sheets of paper, big pencils, felt tips (safety caps only) are useful, plenty of encouragement and praise essential. When the child has drawn a picture write his name on it and encourage him to draw over your letters. He might want you to write something about the picture. Let him tell you what to write, then read it back and let him draw over it. Draw simple patterns for him to copy:

a zigzag

or round and round

## HANDWRITING

Handwriting requires the development of fine muscular movements and very precise control and you must give the child time to develop these. As well as scribbling and drawing, fiddly toys and construction bricks can be useful here.

Left to themselves children find their own way of making letter shapes but it is very important to teach them the correct formation from the beginning, otherwise they have to alter the way they write later at school and this can be surprisingly difficult.(Appendix One shows the formation and direction of letters.) At this pre-school stage very few children develop sufficient fine motor control to write properly and it is probably better just to let them scribble or write over your letters. Always check that the pencil or chalk is held correctly.

## TALKING BOOKS

Fairly new on the market are talking books, well-known stories produced as illustrated books with accompanying audio tapes. The child listens to the story while following it in the book. Probably, at first, he will just look at the pictures but at a later stage can follow the text and join in. They can be repeated over and over again - and usually are. Some libraries have them.

## TELEVISION

There are excellent programmes on television for pre-school children which not only provide talking points and vicarious experiences but also tell stories, teach songs and rhymes and talk about words, letters and sounds. These can be very useful but watch them with your child and talk about them afterwards. They may have good ideas to follow up.

# KEY POINTS FROM CHAPTER 1

1. Talk to your baby from birth. Stimulate his senses. Give him quiet time alone as well as lots of socialising.

2. Encourage your child to talk. Praise his efforts. Give him experiences which he will want to talk about. Listen to him and answer his questions. Teach him rhymes and songs. Read to him.

3. Make the bedtime story an enjoyable ritual. Repeat favourite stories over and over again. Talk about the pictures. Point to words as you read them. Teach your child to treat books with respect. Give him many opportunities for pretend reading.

4. Play is a good thing. Encourage it. Children who play hard work hard. Give time for social and solitary play.

5. Teach your child to recognise individual words and sentences by using flash cards, starting with his own name. Play games with them. Praise lavishly. Point out words around you.

6. Talk about letters and sounds incidentally, introducing them gradually. Do not, at this stage, attempt to 'sound out' words.

7. Writing should arise spontaneously in the form of scribbling, developing slowly into recognisable letters. Again, the child should learn his own name first (written in lower case printing with a capital letter at the beginning. Make sure that letters are formed correctly.

8. Talking books and good pre-school programmes can be useful in promoting literacy. Vet them first then enjoy them together.

# 2

# FACTORS INVOLVED IN READING SUCCESS

## WANTING TO READ

Almost all children can learn to read and the major factor in their success is their burning desire to do so. Children learn best when they are eager to try and a positive emotional attitude to reading on the part of the child coupled with an encouraging, enthusiastic attitude on the part of the adult gives enormous impetus to the whole process. The child who really wants to read, will read.

The last chapter dealt with how to encourage this attitude in the very young child. Suffice to say here that the more the child sees reading as an adult activity the more he will want to emulate it. (This explains to a considerable degree the difficulties encountered in school by many children who come from bookless homes where reading is not valued.) The child who already enjoys books, who goes to them independently and asks to have stories read to him is already highly motivated towards drawing meaning from print for himself.

## ADULT ATTITUDES

While the child's attitudes and motivation are of prime importance, those of the adults around him can have very definite effects. Children need encouragement and support so parents should show an interest, praise his efforts and keep his confidence high. Finding the right stance between encouragement and pushing too hard can be difficult and adults need to be sensitive to the effect they have on children. Praise the smallest success, do not expect too much and never express disappointment - a sure way to make the child feel a failure. Supportive adults can work wonders for a child's fragile self image. Showing your confidence in his abilities will almost certainly increase his self confidence and improve his performance.

## INNATE FACTORS

Certain predisposing factors for reading success are innate and therefore beyond the child's or parent's control. Good sight and hearing, for example, are inborn physical qualities. Nevertheless, where there is less than perfect hearing or vision, steps should be taken to ensure they are improved as much as possible - and quickly. It is not unusual to find cases of reading failure which can be traced back to hearing loss at a critical time in language development. This may have gone unrecognised and led to defective speech and poor expressive powers, whereas fitting gromets or taking other palliative action could have improved hearing at a vital time. Similarly vision needs checking if there are any doubts about it and speech defects remedied as far as possible.

## INTELLIGENCE

General intelligence has an effect on reading as it does on almost everything else. A highly intelligent child will make the connection between marks on a page and words that tell a story more quickly than his less able peers but that does not mean to say that less intelligent children will not learn to read or that every high I.Q. child will do so easily. Other factors such as emotional attitudes can have a tremendous effect.

## HEALTH

Good general health is an added plus. Children who feel well, who are adequately fed, sheltered and rested are far more likely to do well academically than those who are ill, poorly nourished and lacking sleep. Many studies have shown that healthy, well-cared for children do better at school than those from less fortunate homes. There are always exceptions, of course, but ensuring your child is physically fit and well looked after will give him the best possible chance.

## MATURITY

The child's maturity is important too. Whereas at one time it was thought that children needed to reach a mental age of six to be capable of learning to read, now we know that they can and do read at a much younger stage. However, they need to be sufficiently mature to:

listen for fifteen minutes or more

concentrate for at least fifteen minutes

retell a simple story correctly

play constructively

play alone

co-operate reasonably and

be fairly self reliant.

Sight and hearing need to be developed to the stage where the child can discriminate between similar sounds (thing\sing, let\net, gate\cake) and between visual patterns in pictures, shapes and words. To a certain extent children can be trained to do this, particularly if it is fun. Draw two simple faces, one smiling, the other with the mouth turned down.

28

Ask the child if the pictures are the same or different. If he says different, ask in what way. If he says the same, tell him to look again. Draw attention to the mouth. If he still thinks they are the same (genuinely) he is not ready for reading. Similarly, show a cardboard circle alongside a cardboard triangle. Ask if they are the same or different. Make a set of circles, triangles and squares and ask the child to sort them. Children enjoy sorting, whether it be sweets into their various colours, buttons or bricks. Playing with a toy farm he sorts the animals - sheep in this field, cows in that. Ask him to arrange his books on the shelf, big ones that end, small ones this.(In reality recognising words is all about discriminating between shapes, seeing likenesses and differences, holding the idea of a shape in the mind.) Another way to help a child do this is to draw a simple picture, turn over the paper and ask the child to draw the same thing. Then compare the two. Put three toys on a tray. Ask the child to close his eyes and remove one. See if he can tell you what is missing. There are many, many ways to make this kind of learning fun but make sure there is plenty of laughter and absolutely no criticism .

## STORY BOOK LANGUAGE

When children are read to on a regular basis and have contact with many books and stories they develop a knowledge of book language, the different vocabulary of make believe. Certain words and phrases used in stories rarely crop up in conversation - 'ogre', 'thereupon', 'enchanted', 'deep in the forest', 'filled with wonder', - and children with an appreciation of this special story language have already developed strategies for handling written as opposed to spoken words. They develop an ability to follow a plot, to create imaginative images, to find meanings and to predict outcome. The whole purpose of reading is to extract meaning, the reader decoding and reconstructing a message from the writer. The printed word is not speech written down but another system of communication, a medium which has its own particular feel and character. Children with story book experience intuitively internalise and understand this and search for meaning when they come to read for themselves, rather than just recognise words.

## BROAD LANGUAGE DEVELOPMENT

The importance of the child's own language development has already been stressed, exciting experiences, conversation with adults and questions answered resulting in a wide vocabulary and an ability to use words to convey thoughts and emotions, to reflect on the past and to predict the future A variety of experiences and the opportunity to describe and review them not only extends vocabulary but enables a child to hold ideas and images in his mind which he can refer back to at any time. Such children are already predisposed to reading and their intuitive and extensive use of language is a major factor in reading success.

## CONVENTIONS OF PRINT

A knowledge of the conventions of print is an added bonus. If a child already understands what print looks like, its direction, what it represents, if he has the concept of words, letters and spaces firmly established, he has overcome a major hurdle. If, further, he understands different letter forms (upper and lower case), has some knowledge of punctuation and understands the consistency principle (that words always have the same spelling), then he is well on his way to literacy.

# KEY POINTS FROM CHAPTER 2

Major factors in reading success are that:

1. The child wants to read

2. He sees it as an adult activity which he wishes to copy

3. Adults encourage and support his efforts

4. He has normal sight and hearing

5. He is of normal or higher intelligence

6. He has good general health

7. He has reached a sufficient level of maturity

8. He has an understanding of book language from which he can extract meaning and which he appreciates as another medium of communication

9. His own language is sufficiently developed

10. He understands the conventions of print.

# 3

# METHODS OF TEACHING READING

## SHIFTS OF FOCUS

Over the years most parents (and a great many teachers) have been confused by the various methods of teaching reading which have come and gone with monotonous regularity. Extreme shifts of focus have occurred during the past fifty years, with teachers expected to change their whole approach (often against their better judgement) in order to jump on the latest band wagon, to follow the latest trend, the 'new ' discovery which is supposed to cure all ills and lead to a universally literate society. None do. None are perfect. The fact is that most children learn to read whatever the method used, even despite it. Good, intuitive teachers find their own individual ways of teaching reading, built up over years of experience and any method is only as good as the teacher using it. This chapter gives an overview of the various approaches to teaching reading, past and present, simplifying the jargon which parents may hear in schools but not necessarily understand.

## THE ALPHABET APPROACH

The Romans are thought to have used an alphabet approach with wooden blocks to teach the letters of the alphabet. Recognition of individual letters came first, followed by the formation of letters into words, then words into sentences. Medieval monks on the other hand became literate by learning prayers and religious texts by heart, gradually recognising the words they repeated so often then eventually identifying letters which made up words.

When compulsory education started in Britain in the late nineteenth century classes were huge and reading considered to be of prime importance so uniform methods were used. Children began by learning letter names then recited the spellings of selected words over and over again until they knew them. The same sentences were repeated day after day until most of the children in the class could recite the whole book. Then they would all begin on the next one. As a method of teaching this had very obvious failings. Not only was reading seen as an entirely mechanical process but little recognition was taken of individual differences and abilities. Eventually this alphabetic approach was dropped and the phonic method took its place.

## THE PHONIC APPROACH

The phonic approach is based not on letter names but on sounds. Children are expected to learn the sound of each individual letter first then to blend or 'sound them out' to make words. Initially they are taught the common sounds, with only one given for each letter - a as in apple, b as in bed, c as in cat etc. -and are taught regular words only so that these can be combined successfully as in the famous 'cat sat on mat'. Its major weakness is that to begin with it gives just twenty-six out of the actual sixty plus sounds the alphabet letters make and severely limits the reading material which is artificial and contrived. Irregular words have to be learnt separately or left out altogether (commonly occurring words like 'the' cannot be sounded out using the twenty-six sounds) and too many small words are used so that all semblance to a proper story is removed. The very limited vocabulary gives neither excitement nor relevance to the reading material and there is little meaning to be drawn from it.

Unlike Welsh for example, English is not a completely phonetic language and having learnt one set of rules children have to learn all the exceptions which can be thoroughly confusing and demoralising. Many of the words have similar visual patterns (not\hot, hat\mat, wet\met) and children find it difficult to differentiate between them. Too many two- and three-letter words are used and as well as destroying the story element this prevents children from learning words by their contrasting visual patterns.

Many parents who want their children to read early start off by teaching letters and sounds and encourage them to sound out every new word. While some highly intelligent children cope with this successfully, for many it can make reading a drudgery and put them off the whole idea. Further, adult readers do not look at each word on the page in sequence. The eye movements consist of sweeps and pauses, the sweeps recognising groups of words, the fixation pauses allowing their meaning to be absorbed. So it follows that any method which depends on the building up of sounds, syllables and words is in direct opposition to natural eye movements in reading. Rapid reading depends on fast recognition of whole patterns, not a laborious building up of small parts.

Phonic teaching very definitely has a place, though not at the beginning of learning to read. Used in conjunction with a whole word approach it is a useful tool for unravelling new words and identifying differences between them. Looking at the initial letter of a word can assist in its identification and a knowledge of letter sounds is important for spelling. However, just learning the basic twenty-six sounds is not enough and children need to be taught all the blends and digraphs in a structured programme see Appendix Two). Competence in phonics is important and in recent years all too often has been ignored in schools.

## THE SENTENCE METHOD

The sentence method is the complete opposite of the phonic approach and is based on the idea of the sentence as the smallest meaningful unit of language. It begins with the recognition of whole sentences, then of the individual words which make them up, then, very much later of the sounds which create the words. The theory behind it is that children respond to wholes rather than parts and get a visual impression of the complete sentence before they can distinguish separate words. For example:

> I am James

would, according to this theory, be seen by the child as a complete entity with its own characteristic shape. Similarly

> I can jump

> My name is Ben

Longer sentences might follow:

> Edward wants his tea now

> Harry is playing with his train

Only later, say these theorists, does the child realise that bits of one sentence occur in another - I, James, is, his - and he begins to separate the sentences into words. This recognition is encouraged by the use of individual word cards which can be matched to the sentences and by writing, at the children's dictation, under their drawings and paintings.

## THE WHOLE WORD METHOD

The whole word method is similar in that it, too, depends on the recognition of a whole. The unit is not the sentence, nor the letter but the word. Children very quickly learn the shapes of words which have meaning for them (and recognise them upside down and sideways on as well as the right way round.) Many words have distinctive patterns; caterpillar and kangaroo for example are easily remembered, much more so than phonetically simple words like let, met, net, wet.

This method is psychologically sound in that it allows the child quickly to learn words which tell him something. Children can build up quite a large vocabulary of sight words in a surprisingly short time and these can be put together to form sentences. So called 'flash cards' (large cards with one word printed on each held up in front of a group of children for them to recognise) have a bad reputation in schools at the moment but used properly (and especially at home) they can be very useful and great fun. If the words are well chosen and learnt first they enable a child to read right through a book - a tremendous thrill which gives an enormous sense of achievement. This boost in confidence should not be underestimated. The child realises he really can do it and is all the more prepared to make further efforts. Many children who have all but given up using other methods experience a surge of enthusiasm and progress when taught by the whole word approach and less bright children seem to learn more easily this way.

Of course there are some disadvantages, a major one being the masses of very dull 'controlled vocabulary' reading schemes which resulted. The text consisted of carefully chosen words which were used over and over again, often in a very contrived and uninteresting way. Some were quite dire and meaningless supporting the view that a controlled vocabulary impoverished the content of school reading books. However, when compared with the old phonic readers many were a distinct improvement. In fact some managed to produce exciting stories in spite of using a particular set of words and were, and are, very popular with children. As with the sentence method it is essential that eventually letters and sounds are taught.

## READING PROGRAMMES

During the 1950s there was a surge of interest in what were called 'basal' reading programmes from the United States. By now it had become clear that a mixture of methods worked better than one alone so these schemes tried to take the best from each and combine them. They were very prescriptive and teachers were given an actual script to which they were expected to adhere closely. Many found this grossly insulting and in practice organisational chaos was not unusual with groups of children moving round the school to the various teachers responsible for each level. To add to the general disruption these ideas hit Britain at about the same time as open plan classrooms came into vogue and those of us who experienced the utter confusion of those times remember them with horror. The basic ideas were good but they just did not work in practice and within a decade this approach had largely fizzled out.

## INITIAL TEACHING ALPHABET

Another experiment which failed was the initial teaching alphabet. Developed by Sir James Pitman it attempted to create a new alphabet which was phonetically consistent, one symbol always representing one sound. Once children had learned these they could read, and especially write, much more easily. However, having learned and used one set of symbols, two to three years later they had to revert to the traditional alphabet and for many children this caused acute difficulties and confusion so this method too failed to live up to its promise.

## INDIVIDUALISED READING

The idea of individualised reading is credited to Jeanette Veach and although vastly unpopular at first her ideas are widely accepted in schools now. The theory is that reading schemes as such are completely unnecessary (if not downright harmful) and that children can learn to read successfully and happily from ordinarily published children's books which they choose for themselves and read at their own pace, in other words 'real' books. As with most new ideas there was general confusion and lack of understanding in schools at first and shock\horror on the part of parents, understandably so. Instead of working through a reading scheme, visibly progressing from one level to another, suddenly their children were bringing home books well beyond their reading ability one day, far too easy the next - apparently being able to choose exactly what they wanted. (Some schools at this stage had not got round to explaining to parents that the books were meant to be shared with them and that the children were not expected to know every word.) A great many teachers resented these new ideas, genuinely disturbed at the thought of abdicating responsibility for a child's learning from the teacher to the child himself. The teacher was no longer expected to instruct but to enable.

## DEVELOPMENTAL LEARNING

Gradually the approach based on developmental learning and the shared book experience has spread throughout our schools and has been the cause of much distress and misunderstanding. It has also been the means of great achievement. The basic theory is that we should respect the learning potential of all children and accept that children will teach themselves within a properly supportive environment. The whole idea of children competing against one another they say, must be obliterated and all learning must be highly individual and entirely self regulated. (In other words children learn when they want to learn and they will want to when they are ready to do so.) Parents and teachers are expected to have faith in children's ability to teach themselves.

Schools aim at enriching children's language experiences by the shared enjoyment of stories, songs and rhymes and encourage spoken language, immersing their pupils in an environment which will lead to the development of literacy. For teachers this means putting stress on child watching and monitoring, being aware of when to support and when to leave alone. Tremendous demands are made on teachers using this method and it is an unfortunate fact that large classes and insufficient funds can prevent it from succeeding. With a class of twenty, a talented, sensitive and exceptionally hard-working teacher plus an abundance of good materials and support it can work wonderfully well. Unfortunately few of our schools are able to provide these conditions.

## KEY POINTS FROM CHAPTER 3

1.  Most children learn to read irrespective of the method used.

2.  The alphabetic approach involves learning the names of the letters first then letters are made into words and words into sentences.

3.  The phonic approach is based on sounds. Children learn the twenty-six common sounds of the individual letters of the alphabet then the blends and digraphs. They are required to roll these together in the order they occur in a word, 'sounding out' the word in order to identify it. Reading materials can be unreal and contrived. Many words cannot be sounded out. Does not encourage recognising words by their differing visual patterns. Phonic teaching essential but at a much later stage.

4.  In the sentence method sentences are the meaningful units. Children learn to recognise them initially as whole later coming to see them as made up of words, then words of letters.

5.  The whole word or 'look and say' approach is similar but with the word as the unit. Both encourage recognition through visual pattern and are psychologically sound. Children readily learn words and sentences which hold meaning for them. A disadvantage was that some unexciting, controlled vocabulary reading schemes resulted. Learning sounds later on is necessary.

6.  'Basal' reading programmes tried to combine the best of all methods but were too prescriptive and chaotic in practice.

7.  The initial teaching alphabet was an attempt to create a new English alphabet which was entirely phonetic. The child learnt to read and write using this but later had to change to the traditional alphabet, confusing many.

8. Individualised reading allowed children to choose their own reading materials from a large array of generally published children's literature. Reading schemes were out, 'real' books were in.

9. Developmental reading or the shared book experience arose from this. Responsibility for his own learning is given to the child. Teachers are required to enable rather than to instruct. Schools are expected to provide the right environment for children to develop literacy as and when they are ready. Great demands are made of teachers. This method is developmentally sound but can only be expected to succeed for all children when classes are small.

# 4

# BOOKS

---

## CHOOSING BOOKS

Children's books are better now than they have ever been. The advent of 'real' books in the classroom gave a boost to the production of high quality children's literature and shops everywhere are full of beautifully illustrated books for children of all ages and all stages. This chapter does not intend to list them. Such choices are personal and subjective and parents and children need to look around and choose for themselves. It does, however, suggest ideas which adults might consider when buying books for children and further considers what might be suitable for various age groups.

## SMALL CHILDREN

For babies and very small children cloth, plastic or cardboard books are ideal. They are easy for little fingers to handle and are less destructible. There are some very attractive padded cloth picture books around with simple, colourful illustrations, just one object per page (a ball or teddy for example), items children can see around them and recognise instantly. These books are soft and squeezable and babies like the feel as well as the look of them.

Cardboard pages are much easier to turn than the paper variety and lots of these are available. Often they come in the shape of the theme e.g. duck-shaped for a story about a duck.. These books can take a lot of wear and not look tatty and are a good introduction to reading together, turning pages and looking at pictures. The small 'chunkie' books made of thick board remain popular from babyhood right through the toddler stage. Children love their tiny size, easy to hold and 'read' on their own. They are easy to turn, easy to tuck under a pillow or in a pocket. With these, as with all books for young children, look for good, clear print (if there is any) in lower case ('small') letters and good, clear, realistic pictures.

One one-and-a-half-year-old grandson takes the taste for realism a stage further. His very favourite book is one based on actual photographs. Each page has a clear photograph, say of a dog or a cow, with just the one word printed clearly beneath it. Even very small children can point to the picture and try to say the word, usually drawing ecstatic praise from those around him. When they are older they still return to these loved books and can use them as picture dictionaries.

## PICTURES

In early books pictures are as important as words and at an older age a lot of enjoyment can be had from those with no words at all. Look for 'busy' pictures - a lot of detail and several things going on at the same time. These can lead to much pleasurable discussion, exploring possibilities, drawing conclusions, predicting outcome.

"I wonder what's in that parcel?"

"Where do you think they are going?"

"What do you think will happen next?"

"Why is everybody wearing a coat except that little boy?"

Such pictures can be useful for developing concentration and children often notice things adults might miss resulting in a torrent of questions.

"Why does that little girl look sad?"

"What makes the bouncy castle bounce?"

"Why is that baby wearing one shoe?"

"Why is candy floss fluffy?"

One particular series has a tiny duck on every page, often in very unlikely places and as you turn the page children rush to find it first with cries of, "There's the duck."

## INTERACTIVE BOOKS

Some books for small children are interactive in that they require certain actions in order to get the most from them. There are sound books, (press the picture of the cow and it says moo, or the train and hear it rushing by), feelie books, ("I am a rabbit. Feel my soft tail.""I am a chimpanzee. Feel my hairy chest.") and the ever popular lift the flap books. There are a great many of these and most are excellent. Children love lifting the flaps to find Ted or Spot and do so over and over again. They are expensive and easily spoiled so this has to be weighed against the pleasure they give.

## REPETITION

Children enjoy books with a repetitive strain and rhyming verse, from the traditional

"Run, run, as fast as you can
You can't catch me. I'm the gingerbread man."

to the more contemporary

"No, no, Charlie Rascal." and

"Each peach pear plum."

There are some excellent contemporary children's authors producing very high quality children's books which will be enjoyed by adults too.

## STORIES WITH A MORAL/STORY TAPES

At around the ages of three to five children begin to like stories with a moral. They prefer right to triumph, rules to be obeyed. Books such as Martin Waddel's Farmer Duck are very satisfying for this age group. Story tapes also come into their own at this stage. At first children may prefer just to listen to the tape while quietly playing and only later refer to the book itself.

## QUALITY AND PRICE

Books do not have to be expensive to be good. The major supermarkets all have their own series of children's books which are of very high quality and at less than £1.50 each are extremely good value. Nor does one have to bend to peer pressure and buy the currently popular stories concerning a certain postman, steam locomotives or a little nodding man. There are plenty of others available which could prove to be even more enjoyable and satisfying. A few hours browsing (preferably alone) among the vast array of children's literature can be both enlightening and pleasurable.

A lot of older books are back in fashion and it is undoubtedly true that if parents have known and loved  particular books when young themselves then they will pass on this enthusiasm to their children. However it is important that adults avoid setting a child against a book just because of a personal aversion to it. Communicate your preferences but not your prejudices.

## READING SCHEMES

So far this chapter has dealt with informal reading books for young children, stories, rhymes and illustrations to entertain and amuse.

However, some parents may be looking for reading text books specifically intended to help children learn to read, in other words reading schemes. There are many to choose from and they fall into three major categories:

## `REAL' BOOKS

Firstly there are the 'real' books - collections of high quality children's literature intended to be used in the shared reading or developmental approach. They work on the assumption that children should be presented with powerful reading matter with fantasy and imagination called into play and stories reaching well into the realms of the impossible. The stories should be so compelling that children are prepared to make tremendous efforts to read them for themselves.

## BOOKS BASED ON EVERYDAY EXPERIENCES

Then there are those which use everyday experiences as a basis for reading materials. The child finds his own life reflected in print, the world as he knows it. The texts are relevant to his own experiences, the vocabulary familiar and likely to be used by the child himself. Most of the schemes try to avoid situations and events restricted to one particular social class (some fail) and disclose a child's view of the world rather than that of the adult. The stories turn on everyday happenings with realistic outcomes and believable events.

## CONTROLLED VOCABULARY SCHEMES

Lastly there are controlled vocabulary schemes based on the look and say approach to reading. Their basic idea is that the repetition of known words gives a child confidence and allows him to read right through a book at an early stage. New words are introduced gradually and the reading material is carefully graded so that the child progresses but retains confidence. It is argued that the most important factor in children's reading is their initial attitude and that if a child succeeds early on he is more likely to persist. If there are too many new words on the page he might become discouraged and lose confidence. Once one page is mastered he is faced with another equally daunting. The theory is that if you build in success from the beginning, using known words over and over again, children will find reading a pleasurable activity and want to continue with it. These schemes certainly encourage those who have previously failed and work well with less able children. However, it is difficult to write great literature with a controlled vocabulary and the stories sometimes seem contrived to fit round the words rather than the other way round.

## LIBRARIES

Once children are reading well they have the whole range of children's books to choose from and it is wise to let them make their own choices. Join them to the local library at a very young age and take them there regularly, allowing plenty of time to browse and choose. Most libraries are well stocked with children's literature and will gladly give suggestions and advice. For families who cannot afford to buy books libraries are a godsend and children can have a constant supply of new stories. If, further, parents are seen to choose books for their own pleasure and to read them at home their children have a personal model to emulate and are likely to develop a love of books for life.

## KEY POINTS FROM CHAPTER 4

1. Cloth, plastic and cardboard books are ideal for small children.

2. Pictures are as important as words in early books. Talk with children about the pictures and encourage questions.

3. Interactive books are fun - sound books, feelies and lift the flap.

4. Children like repetition. Look for books which use this.

5. Discover the many excellent contemporary authors.

6. Stories with a moral and story tapes are very popular between ages three to five.

7. Supermarket own series are inexpensive and of good quality.

8. Reading text books come in three categories:

a) ' real' books - powerful stories involving fantasy and imagination,

b) those based on everyday experiences and using the child's vocabulary,

c) controlled vocabulary books using a specific set of words.

9. Use the local library - parents as well as children.

# 5

# STARTING SCHOOL

## PREPARATION

Starting school is one of the great adventures of a child's life. It can be a satisfying and exciting experience or a terrible ordeal. Either way it denotes an end to a child's freedom. For the next sixty years or so he will be bound by the constraints of education and employment. Probably never again will he be able to choose so consistently what he does and how he does it. Some parents seem not to realise the enormity of the step. From being part of a small group and used to small spaces an unprepared child can be plunged into a huge room (to him) among a crowd of completely unknown children without the adults he knows and loves best. Fortunately this nightmare scenario rarely occurs nowadays. Parents and schools are wise enough to know that preparation for school must be a long and careful process.

The first or only child in a family is likely to need more in the way of preparation than subsequent children. For them the pattern is set and they will know all about school from their siblings. From a young age they will have seen brothers and sisters coming and going to and from school, will know it as a place and have some idea of what goes on there.

They will probably know what a 'teacher' is and what a 'classroom' looks like and they will almost certainly have been in the playground. The situation is very different for the first or only child who may have no idea what a 'school' is.

From pushchair days the wise parent starts pointing out the local school, perhaps arranging to walk past at playtime and watch the children play.

Talk about it as an exciting place where children learn all kinds of interesting things, where it is possible to make lots of new friends. Read together some of the wonderful school preparation books that are available and talk about your own schooldays. Once you have decided for sure which school you want your child to attend ask if you and the child can be shown round during school time and check that arrangements will be made for an induction period. Some schools have children in for a story time at first, or one afternoon a week once they are four years old, others have just occasional visits, some a whole term of part time attendance. If it is the school's policy, ask for a home visit. This will give you, the child and the teacher an opportunity to talk quietly together, to answer any questions and get to know each other.

## PLAYGROUPS AND NURSERY SCHOOLS

Many children attend playgroups or nurseries from around three years old and those who do will already be used to spaces larger than home and groups bigger than the family. They will have been left in the care of other adults and will know from experience that although parents may leave them temporarily they will come back. They will be used to the company of other children and will already be learning appropriate social behaviour. However, attending nurseries or playgroups which are not well run can be counter productive and parents should check them out very carefully indeed. The rowdy behaviour allowed in some playgroups will not be tolerated in school and it is difficult for children who have been used to tearing round a hall on a trike or grabbing toys from other children to accept the quieter routines of school.

## EXPLANATIONS

Certain aspects of school need to be explained carefully. For example it may be very strange to a child to be told to, "Get undressed for P.E." Often they do just that. After all, no-one told them they were supposed to keep on their vests and pants and who is P.E. anyway? Another teacher? From a child's point of view it can all be very confusing and although this may seem a far cry from learning to read and write in fact it has a very definite bearing. A confused and unhappy child cannot take full advantage of the best teaching whereas one who has come happily to school with high expectations and a knowledge of school routines can settle quickly and confidently. By talking enthusiastically about school from the very beginning parents can help their children gain effectively from it.

## THE MODERN CLASSROOM

Almost certainly parents will find schooling nowadays to be very different from their own. The modern primary class is likely to be a bustling hive of activity, with children working individually or in small groups at different tasks rather than as a teacher-directed unit. The teacher may not be visible immediately and certainly not sitting at a desk (there may not even be a teacher's desk). Children's tables and chairs will be in groups or 'work stations' and probably there will be a comfortable carpeted area where the whole class can gather for discussions and corporate activities. In the Infant classroom there will be plenty of toys, probably a well equipped house corner and a dressing up box as well as other activities to encourage language development. Talking and listening will be as important as reading and writing and children will be expected to learn by doing and observing. There should be many good quality books in a pleasant reading area, the classroom walls covered with sensitively displayed children's work produced individually and in groups. The whole emphasis should be on providing a stimulating environment and enabling children to develop skills and positive attitudes to learning.*

---

\* If your child's school shows little resemblance to this model find out why and question poor provision. Every child and every parent has the right to expect schooling in line with the latest educational beliefs.

It is likely that the 'integrated day' system will be in operation. Instead of distinct 'lessons' at specific times, children have a set of tasks to complete during the day and may work at just one for an hour or more. On one day a child may do no maths at all, the next he might spend most of his work time on it. The teacher allows the child to be self-directed, not in competition with others but developing at his own rate. The school will probably be using the real books approach to reading and children will be encouraged to choose books to take home for shared reading. (See chapter three.)

## PARENTAL AND TEACHER CONCERNS

Some parents can find this difficult to accept. They want to know that their children are doing as well or better than others. For most, their main concern with schooling is that their children become literate and it disturbs them when children come home with books they cannot read. Even when told that all the words are not expected to be correct and that children are meant just to draw out the overall meaning, parents still worry. Some schools produce explanatory booklets upholding the psycholinguistic view that reading is not a matter of knowing the words first and then getting the meaning but vice versa. However, this remains an area of great concern for parents and for some teachers. It is asking much of them where there are large classes. They have to monitor each individual child closely and a lot of teachers are just not capable of doing so with thirty-plus children. Whilst the theory is good it is not always properly implemented. Indeed, the most recent HMI report stated that 25% of all infant teaching was unsatisfactory. (This rose to 30% in junior schools.) Basically it is literacy without instruction and many teachers have been made to feel guilty about instructing children at all. The disadvantage of discovery learning is that children do not always learn everything they should and sometimes need instruction.

# SHARING SESSIONS

At some time during the day the class will gather together for a 'sharing' session. Often a favourite story is read and the teacher may have a large book version of the tale or have enlarged one herself so that everyone can follow the words. This will be very like the bedtime story situation with considerable interaction between adult and children. Members of the class may later reproduce these stories themselves, usually working in groups and making ultra large versions for display.

# NAME CARDS

Very soon after he starts school each child will be given a name card and encouraged first to trace over and later to copy it. (Hopefully parents will have already familiarised him with his name in lower case letters.) He will probably be painting and drawing, the teacher writing words beneath at his dictation. These may be displayed at school or brought home. Show that you value them and put them up where everyone can admire them.

# PROJECTS

Projects or centres of interest are the bases of much work and activity in the classroom. Parents may well be asked to contribute, by finding a picture of their child as a baby for a project on growth for example or arranging a weekend walk to collect leaves and acorns. When parents are enthusiastic about these activities it confirms their value and encourages a child to be interested too.

# COMPUTERS

Computers are being used with young children more and more and there are very few schools, if any, without them. With no preconceived ideas, children are able to handle computers expertly within a very short time. There are excellent programmes to reinforce maths and language skills, many readily available for use at home. Children have been drawing up charts at school for may years, mapping heights, colour of eyes, favourite animals or sandwich fillings. Now they can produce them via the computer, keying in information and finally printing out the finished chart. Computers are the learning tools of the future and it is rare to find a child who is not excited by and eager to use them.

## JUDGING PROGRESS

With competition discouraged and none of the old reading levels against which to judge him, parents are anxious to know whether their child is making normal progress. The class teacher should be consulted about this and parents would be well advised to discuss with the teacher any doubts or worries. Generally speaking a child should be happily settled in school within a matter of weeks, be confident and at ease in his new environment by the first half term and be showing an interest in books and writing within a month or two. By the time he is six he should have some sight words which he recognises instantly and begin to use sounds to help with spelling and unknown words. He should use context clues and be prepared to guess a word from its context and be able to retell a known story. He should hold a pencil properly and be able to write a few words from memory as well as copy write. By the time children leave the infant school at seven plus most will be reading and writing on their own and know the individual letter sounds and a few blends and digraphs. He should be able to spell simple words and use full stops and capital letters correctly. Above all, he should be enthusiastic about learning. Infant school establishes the pattern of success and failure which persists right through the junior stage. Children must succeed in the infants and develop the right attitudes to learning. The importance of early education cannot be overestimated. Infant school provision has a lasting effect on children and it is up to parents to choose their child's first school wisely.

# KEY POINTS FROM CHAPTER 5

1.  It is important to prepare children for school, especially first children. Talk about school, visit, take advantage of any induction programme and home visits.

2.  Good playgroups and nurseries are an excellent preparation for school. Children realise that although parents leave them with other adults they will return.

3.  Explain all aspects of school, looking at them from the child's point of view.

4.  The modern infant classroom enables children to develop skills and positive attitudes through discovery and developmental learning methods. Classrooms are equipped to encourage talking and listening, individual and corporate activities. Children are self motivated rather than teacher directed.

5.  The integrated day allows children to continue specific tasks for as long as they want rather than have to stop at the end of a lesson.

6.  Parents need to understand how the real books\shared reading approach works.

7.  Some teachers, especially those with large classes, fail properly to implement this approach.

8.  Children sometimes need instruction but teachers have been made to feel guilty about providing it.

9.  Daily sharing sessions are similar to the bedtime story situation.

10. Children begin writing by tracing over name cards and dictating words to go under their pictures.

11.  Parents are expected to contribute to and support projects and to be enthusiastic about them.

12.  Computers are being used widely in infant schools and provide an exciting new way to learn.

13.  Parents are advised to discuss their child's progress with the class teacher on a regular  basis.

14.  Normal progress:

By first half term: settled and confident in school,
showing an interest in books and writing.

By six years old:  knows some sight words,
begins to use letter sounds as clues,
guesses words from context,
retells a known story,
holds pencil properly,
writes a few words from memory.

By seven plus:  reads and writes on his own
knows letter sounds, some
blends and digraphs, spells
simple words, uses full stops,
capital letters, shows enthusiasm for learning.

15.  Success in the infant school establishes a pattern for success throughout schooling.

# 6

# BEGINNING TO WRITE

## COMPLEXITIES

Writing and spelling are considerably more difficult than speaking and reading. Not only has a child to hold an idea and the shape of a sentence in his mind. At the same time he has to use fine muscular, motor control of his hand and a sophisticated hand\eye co-ordination. Control of large muscular movements comes first in infancy with finer control developing later and demanding intense effort, concentration and practice. Add to that the vagaries of the English language and it becomes clear that the development of writing and spelling cannot be expected to keep pace with reading in these early years.

As well as having to master the complicated task of thinking out sentences the child has to learn handwriting and spelling if he is to produce written rather than spoken language. There are vast differences between the two and writing does not develop as naturally as speech. Babies are surrounded by human voices and know the sounds of speech from their earliest days. Only much later do they become aware of writing as marks which have meaning. Speech is a social act, usually involving two or more people, whereas writing is a solitary activity, the writer alone with his thoughts, generating ideas for an audience absent at the moment of creation. This abstract aspect of writing can be a difficult hurdle for children to overcome. An idea can be verbalised immediately whereas writing it out can be a laborious process involving thinking out the sentences, attempting spelling and physically marking the thoughts upon a page.

## THE ENGLISH WRITING SYSTEM

Our writing system is not the easiest in the world. It is alphabetic with twenty-six letters, each with two shapes (upper and lower case) and many variations in the way these are formed. Our system goes from left to right, the words separated by spaces and together forming sentences. These sentences are arranged in paragraphs. Punctuation marks are used to shape and clarify meaning, italics mark words that are stressed. Unlike other European languages English has no written accents but there are sets of signs denoting numerals, words and abbreviations (2, &, Mrs) and an apostrophe to denote possession and contractions e.g. Jane's dog, didn't, he's. Where rules exist often there are exceptions - scarf\scarves but roof\roofs. The English writing system has a complicated history and the effects of Anglo Saxon, Norman French, Latin and Greek combine to create its unique form. Small wonder that getting to grips with written English can be a daunting task.

## FIRST STAGES

Most children begin with scribbling which represents words. Probably the child's own name will be the first word he can write from memory and for a while he will depend on the teacher or parent as scribe, saying the words he wants written down and trying to copy over them. Encourage your child to talk about the pictures he paints and draws, writing under them at his dictation. If he tells you a story, ask if he would like you to write it down. Make a book together of 'John's Stories' or 'Paul's Poems' and read them together. When friends and relatives have birthdays even very small children can write their cards. Nobody minds a few mistakes and most recipients are touched to know that the child has made an effort. Thank you letters are greatly appreciated and writing to friends and relatives should be encouraged. Let the learner-writer be in charge of the family diary and write in appointments and events, mistakes and all.

## INITIAL ENTHUSIASM/CORRECT SPELLING

Some children get the story writing bug early and fill pages with strangely spelt words which they read convincingly. Heap on the praise and encouragement and accept approximations of words with equanimity. Children cannot be expected to get to grips with our peculiar English spelling straight away and it may be two to three years before they are accurate to any great extent. If children have something they want to write about, encourage them to do so whether or not they can spell the words. Spelling is important and must be learned but enthusiasm is easily squashed and it is more important initially to be putting ideas on paper than to be struggling over the spelling of each individual word.

## LEARNING TO SPELL

When it comes to learning how to spell as a separate and definite activity, begin with the most commonly used words, (see Appendix Three). If you see a wrongly spelt word occurring over and over again (wos for was, nite for night) make a point of teaching it correctly before the mistake becomes an ingrained habit. Many words are learnt by constant use and the child soon knows when a word does not look right. The Delcroy system trains children to make mental pictures of words before writing them. They spend a few seconds visualising the word which is then covered. They write as much of it as they can remember then the word is uncovered and the spelling checked. This system is widely used in schools and generally referred to as 'Look. Cover. Write. Check.' It is the preferred way for children to learn their individual spellings.

Often letter names are introduced at this stage and attention drawn to the way symbols combine to make words. The complexity of English spelling and the variations of regional accents should be acknowledged from the beginning but there are regular word patterns and rules which can be taught to encourage correct spelling. (See Appendix Four) Children are more successful at spelling if they use written language frequently and for many purposes, if they are interested in language and if they ask questions about words that puzzle them.

It is a good idea to use a properly structured spelling scheme and to make a point of encouraging children to learn a few new words regularly - just five words each week would ensure a child would know all the key words (Appendix Three) in less than a year. There are various spelling schemes easily available from bookshops. Although it was originally published in 1932, I find Schonell's Essential Spelling List one of the best and have used it effectively for many years. It remains remarkably undated.

Many Infant schools ignore spelling on the grounds that it is an unnecessary complication in the early stages and will be taught in the Junior school anyway. Unfortunately this is not always so and too many children struggle through without ever being taught how to spell. It does them no favours. A child who spells correctly and produces tidy, accurate work has a head start and a distinct advantage over those with erratic spelling. By eight, they should be able to spell all the key words, and more besides. If your child is not spelling correctly by this age, take the problem in hand. Consult the class teacher and, if necessary, start a spelling programme at home. The longer the problem is left after this age, the more mistakes will be compounded. Once incorrect spelling becomes a habit it is difficult to rectify.

**PUNCTUATION**

Similarly with punctuation. In the very recent past, stress on correct punctuation was considered to be old fashioned in some Infant schools. Fortunately the National Curriculum now requires children to use full stops and capital letters correctly by the age of seven and punctuation is gradually creeping back into favour. By the time they are eight children should be using speech marks, commas and paragraphs as well as full stops and capital letters.

# LEGIBLE HANDWRITING

Pride in good handwriting is largely a thing of the past and while no-one would want to return to the days when children were forced to spend hours developing perfect copper plate there is a strong case for ensuring that all children write legibly. It is important that they learn the correct formation and direction of letters from the very beginning. Learning joined writing later on becomes that much easier. Handwriting can be taught as an art form using double lined handwriting exercise books, much like the ones our grandparents used. These are easily available and encourage children to form letters with the correct proportions. If they can be persuaded to take a pride in producing a page of accurate, properly formed and spaced script, then the chances are that they will continue to use good handwriting most of the time. The major problem here is one of motivation. Once writing is used as a separate form rather than as a vehicle of purposeful expression it loses its urgency and substance. Children should write because they have something to say. They should feel an urgent need to communicate through the written word and find satisfaction in doing so. Good hand handwriting is, nevertheless an added bonus. Even the best creative writing will remain unappreciated if it cannot be deciphered. The chart in Appendix One shows the usual formation of letters used when children begin writing.

## SPEECH EXPERIENCES AND CREATIVE WRITING

Children's first attempts at writing rely heavily on their speech experience. Those who have a rich vocabulary based on exciting experiences, much conversation and answered questions, who have listened to and retold a variety of stories and experienced the pleasures of books are likely to want to commit their own feelings and ideas to paper. This has a two way effect. Once speech begins to be written down it makes children more aware of how different speech is used in different situations and enriches their spoken as well as their written language. They begin to use language more comprehensively and effectively, especially when writing stories which use a wider vocabulary than normal conversation.

## ROUGH DRAFTS, CONFERENCES AND THE FINAL COPY

When children are writing creatively the problem of how or whether to correct arises. If a child has spent a lot of time on a piece of work it is unkind and discouraging to go through it and correct every other word. In schools these days teachers overcome this situation by allowing children to write a 'rough draft' first. The child concentrates on the meaning and content of his writing at this stage then, together, he and the teacher hold a 'conference'. The work is discussed and the child encouraged to think about how it could be improved. Incorrect spellings are pointed out at this stage and the child then writes out a final copy which is kept or put up for display. There is a distinct psychological difference in corrections being done in this way rather than by handing in a piece of work, then receiving it back with all the mistakes highlighted. The more modern approach hands control to the child and the teacher is used as an enabler who encourages him to produce the best possible piece of work. It is more time consuming and requires a sensitive attitude on the part of the teacher, not easy when classes are large and teachers overstretched and overstressed.

# KEY POINTS FROM CHAPTER 6

1. Learning to write and spell is more difficult than learning to listen and read.

2. Our formidable writing system further complicates matters.

3. Writing usually begins with scribbling which represents words to children.

4. Do not squash initial enthusiasm for writing by putting too much stress on correct spelling in these very early stages.

5. Teach spelling as a separate activity using one of the excellent spelling schemes available.

6. Encourage regular spelling practice. Aim at a minimum of five new words a week.

7. Punctuation is important. Teach capital letters and full stops, later speech marks, commas and paragraphs.

8. Good handwriting is a useful skill. Encourage it.

9. Children who speak well can write well, each develops the other. Children become more aware of language and its different uses in different situations, the more they write.

10. Allow children to write a rough draft first. Correct only in conference with the child using encouragement and sensitivity.

# 7

# PARENTAL SUPPORT FOR SCHOOLS

## PARENTAL ATTITUDE AND SCHOOL SUCCESS

To a large extent the success or failure of a child's schooling depends upon the attitudes of his parents and parental support is one of the major factors in school success. Experienced teachers can tell within a few weeks which children are likely to do well at school - and not entirely because of their abilities. It soon becomes obvious which families co-operate and support, which object automatically to any school request. Some children always bring the correct dinner money in a named envelope on Monday morning, always bring back their reading books, have named clothes and plimsoll bags. With others it is, "My Mum forgot." or "Dad didn't have any change."

Unfair as this may seem, the children of less caring and less capable parents are often viewed unfavourably compared with those of parents who are more co-operative and supportive. This has nothing to do with the financial standing of the family. In my experience some of the greatest school supporters have been mothers and fathers of single parent families, very badly off in money terms but always ready to show an interest and give their time and enthusiasm. Although the opposite is not always true, certainly I have known quite a few wealthy parents with time and funds available who choose not to support or help in any way.

Even the busiest parents, who genuinely have no time to take part in any school activities can support the ethos of the school by ensuring that their children obey the rules (if there are any), do their homework and generally show respect to the other adults and children. If parents talk dismissively and unfavourably about the school or teachers in front of their children they can hardly be surprised if they, also, develop disrespectful attitudes which will not go down at all well at school.

## HOME/SCHOOL RELATIONS

At one time children were sent to school and left completely in charge of the teachers who were expected to educate them without any involvement of the parents who rarely set foot inside the gates, let alone the building. Things are very different now. Most schools work hard to develop good home\school relations. Often there is considerable contact well before the children start school: home visits, story times, take-home packs and invitations to school events. Parents are welcomed in school at any time and there is generally open access to classrooms and teachers. They are encouraged to air any problems or difficulties and have termly meetings with the class teacher to discuss the child's progress. Often parents are asked to act as assistants in the classroom, hearing children read and helping in other ways. They may be asked to run the school library, to organise sales or run a school tuck shop. Never have parents been allowed such involvement in their children's schooling. There are good reasons for this, educational, professional and financial.

## EDUCATIONAL ASPECTS

Educationally it must be better for pupils to know that their parents and teachers are working together. Children become very fond of their teachers and when there are clashes of opinion or bad feeling between teachers and parents it can upset them considerably. When they present a united front a child can relax in the knowledge that he has all round support and can perform to the best of his ability. If parents take an interest in their child's schooling they show it is important to them. The child then perceives it as important too and works all the harder. Parental enthusiasm washes off on children and when they become involved in projects, outings and lessons children are that much keener and more interested themselves. Psychologists have long known that if the adults around a child are mutually supportive, then that child will do better than if his 'significant others' are at loggerheads.

## PROFESSIONAL ASPECTS

Professionally teachers need parent's help. Modern methods are well nigh impossible for a teacher to carry out alone and help at home is a vital part of children learning to read using the shared reading approach. Classes are far too large for one teacher to cope with and government funding does not allow for properly trained and paid assistants, so parents are used as a cheaper alternative. It can be argued that this is a complete misuse of parental willingness to help and that, in fact, it is perpetuating a shocking situation where teachers are expected to do the impossible. It is not an ideal situation for children. With the best will in the world, most parents are neither trained teachers nor welfare workers and should not be expected to take on the responsibilities of those roles.

## PROBLEMS ARISING FROM PARENTAL HELP

All kinds of difficulties can arise when school helpers talk freely about what goes on in school. It can be very hurtful, for example, to hear a neighbour saying that your child did badly in maths today or was in trouble in school again. Very capable helpers can take on too much responsibility, even taking control from inexperienced teachers but without the necessary knowledge and training. If parents are to be used to support staff professionally, then at the very least they should be offered training by the school and be carefully supervised initially. Both take time and money and it is lack of these that put parents in the classroom in the first place.

## POLITICAL/FINANCIAL ASPECTS

The educational and professional arguments for the presence of parents in schools are those most forcibly put by politicians. However there is a large body of opinion that states that the educational theory follows the financial situation, not precedes it. This has been obvious before in the advent of open plan classrooms (cheaper to build new schools if a few walls are missing), family grouping - meaning mixed age classes - (bigger classes and fewer teachers) and now shared reading (get the parents to teach them at home) and parental help in the classroom (cheaper than employing trained staff).

Government educationalists have tried to produce convincing arguments for all of these and while some undoubtedly have relevance, the main impetus comes from the financial situation. Parents are a cheaper alternative. They give their time freely and enthusiastically. By doing so they save the education budget millions of pounds countrywide. Perhaps it is time to admit that the financial argument for parental help in schools is far more convincing than the educational and professional aspects.

## HOW TO SUPPORT

Parents ask how best they can show that they support their child's school and certainly there are a few golden rules:

1. Before your child starts school read the school booklet and be sure you understand and approve the general ethos of the place and any rules and regulations. It is better not to send your child to that particular school if you disapprove of any major aspect.

2. Find out if parents are involved in the school day, as parent helpers, library assistants etc. If you have the time and inclination offer your services. Apart from being very helpful to the school it is an excellent way to get to know the staff and to find out what really goes on there.

3. Move heaven and earth to attend every school function, from assemblies, Harvest Festivals and Christmas celebrations to Parents' Evening, talks, fetes and book sales.

4. Find out early on how you are meant to help your children at home

and establish a routine that ensures you do exactly what is asked of you.

5. Label everything, shoes, socks, satchels - everything a child takes to school and can be removed from his person.

6. Ensure that you read any notes that are sent home. If a reply is needed, return it promptly.

7. See that your child looks after school property and that the reading book is returned daily and in good condition.

8. Be the first to offer to accompany children on school trips.

9. Ask for an appointment to discuss any problems which may arise.

10. If asked to help with projects etc., try to be enthusiastic.

So far as the 'do nots' are concerned:

1. Never, never make a fuss in front of your child or his classmates, especially to his teacher.

2. If you help in school avoid divulging any sensitive information you may come across and never discuss what other people's children have been up to in school.

3. Similarly, avoid gossip about staff.

4. If you have criticisms about the way the school is run, discuss them privately with the head teacher in the first instance. (The next chapter deals more thoroughly with parental complaints.)

5.  Never speak badly of the school, staff or pupils in front of your child.

Schools really do appreciate the support of parents which makes them feel that their own efforts are appreciated and worthwhile.

## KEY POINTS FROM CHAPTER 7

1. The parent's attitude affects a child's success at school.

2. Children of co-operative parents are viewed more favourably.

3. Ensure that children keep the rules and show respect.

4. Parents are allowed open access to classrooms and are often called upon to help within them.

5. The educational argument for this is that children feel more secure and achieve more when the adults around them work together.

6. Professionally teachers need the help and co-operation of parents if they are to achieve their objectives using modern methods.

7. The main reason for parental help in schools is financial.

8. A list is given of ways parents can best support schools.

9. Also given is a list of 'do nots'.

# 8

# WHEN THINGS GO WRONG

## EMOTIONAL EFFECTS OF FAILURE

From time to time and for no apparent reason certain children fail at school. This is a cause of great concern for everybody involved and rightly so. Parents send their children to school to learn to read and write and failure to do so sets off a cycle which is difficult to break. If a child reaches Junior school unable to read then he has already experienced failure every day for several years. This can produce an emotional attitude to reading which makes success more difficult, no matter how much effort is put into remedying the situation and what starts as a reading difficulty can become a personality problem. Backward readers develop a sense of discouragement and inferiority. It can lead to a hopeless acceptance - 'can't do it'- or an aggressive 'don't care' attitude.

## BACKWARDNESS AND DELINQUENCY

The relationship between backwardness and delinquency is well documented and children often seek to compensate for their lost self respect by anti-social behaviour, gaining the admiration of their peers through naughtiness rather than scholastic achievement. Lost confidence and low self-esteem can result in apathy and boredom or manifest itself in fierce antagonism towards school and learning. Some children feign illness as a reason for not doing well and complain of vague aches and pains, headaches and nausea. However they exhibit this, one thing is certain. No child who is failing to read and write is happy about the situation. Most are desperately unhappy about their lack of progress. Failure to read can have profound psychological and behavioural effects and the older the child the more serious is the problem. Not only is other school work held up but the longer a reading problem persists the more difficult it is to treat.

## THE NATIONAL CURRICULUM

It was hoped that with the advent of the National Curriculum all children would be properly taught and illiteracy would gradually become a thing of the past. The current National Curriculum documents certainly advise all the right things, stressing the importance of experiences, verbal language, exchange of ideas, writing for a specific audience, collaboration etc .Speaking, listening and reflection, the asking of questions and giving of replies are given their due importance, also the role of the teacher as facilitator, supporter, modeller and reader who must ensure continuity, liaison and progression. These are sound and exciting ideas. Indeed, if the National Curriculum as planned were followed by all children it is difficult to imagine that any could fail. However, a great many do fail and recent research has shown that illiteracy is increasing, not decreasing. Certainly, in my own remedial practice, there has been a surge of children coming for help since the advent of the National Curriculum and modern approaches to reading. Television, a changed social situation, modern attitudes have all been named as culprits but schools cannot escape much of the blame. With the best will in the world no teacher, however good, can properly implement the National Curriculum and give every child the attention he needs in classes of more than twenty. Thirty to forty children per class is the norm, which allows the teacher less than five minutes a day in personal contact with each child, not a recipe for maximum progress.

## INFANT/JUNIOR SCHOOLS

Children have to leave the infant school or department when they reach a particular age, not necessarily when then are ready to do so. Often they are not ready for the junior school approach. Junior teachers tend to assume that the pupils coming up to them have reached the expected standards and many, if not most, junior staff are not trained to deal with children who are still at an infant school level of development. The ethos of a junior school is quite different from that of an infants only school. Mostly they are less supportive, less child-centred and less concerned with linguistic development. Many children are just ready to tackle phonics in detail at seven plus but few junior schools teach them systematically, assuming they have been taught already.

## PHYSICAL FACTORS

Even in an adequate teaching situation, however, there will always be a sizeable minority of children who have difficulties in learning to read and this can be due to a variety of problems. Rarely is it traced to one cause only, but rather to a combination of factors which may be physical, social or emotional. Physical factors may include:

poor sight and\or hearing
lack of sleep,
poor nourishment,
septic tonsils\bad teeth,
general ill health and lack of vitality,
hyperactivity.

## SOCIAL FACTORS

Social factors are those concerned with:

poor housing,
illiterate home environment,
little interest from parents,
over-ambitious parents,
boredom,
too much television,
too little conversation\play\experiences.

## EMOTIONAL FACTORS

Emotional factors are those involved in:

anxiety,
insecurity,
unhappiness,
confusion,
fear of failing,
fear of disappointing\displeasing adults.

Normally children can withstand one or two of these factors but when several of them work together the situation becomes much more serious.

## GENERAL INTELLIGENCE

I.Q. or general intelligence also has a bearing on how easily children learn to read. Those of below average intelligence may show late and limited development and may never reach the correct level for their age but they can and do learn to read and, with help, can improve. Children of above or average intelligence who fail may exhibit some of the physical, social or emotional factors already mentioned or may have been confused by changes of teacher and methods or by long absences. Those with exceptionally high I.Q. can have reading problems also. They may have been ready to read at a very early age but have been prevented from doing so, find real difficulty in mastering the mechanics of reading later on. A lot of children, including bright ones, will not try because they are afraid of not succeeding.

## SPECIFIC DIFFICULTIES

Children may have special, specific difficulties in the mental processes required for reading. As well as dyslexia (for more details of this condition see Appendix Five), mixed laterality and dominant eye irregularities have been suggested as possible causes of reading problems.

These conditions need investigation by an expert. Whether or not dyslexia is as prevalent as some would have us believe, any child with a reading problem is in a serious situation. The causes should be thoroughly investigated and remedial action taken promptly.

## MEASURING SUCCESS

In these days of non-competition it is difficult for a parent to know if a child is performing satisfactorily. When graded readers were used it was easy to see whether a pupil was at the expected level and how he compared with his peers. With modern approaches parents have no yardstick by which to measure their child's success. Recently introduced national tests at seven, eleven and fourteen should remedy this situation but remain to be proved. Meanwhile the only sure way to find out is to ask the teacher. Fortunately most schools have regular parent consultations which give the opportunity of airing any worries. Take advantage of these and make a list beforehand of any questions you want answered.

## PARENTAL COMPLAINTS

If your child is unhappy at school and not performing well there must be a reason and it is up to the parents to find out what that reason is. (Any good school will want to know why also.) However, it is very easy for a parent to believe that a child is being 'got at' by a teacher when he comes crying home with a tale of woe. With a rush of protective instincts the parent is ready to take off and fight on the child's behalf. Do pause for thought and take a few deep breaths first. While it is a natural reaction to protect one's young, a belligerent parent storming into school to make a complaint just spells trouble maker to the staff. If there is a problem ask for an appointment to discuss it with the class teacher and the head teacher, without the child being present. Usually they are only too willing to help.

Once any problems have been aired, expect an improvement. If there is none within a week or two ask for another appointment with the head teacher and state that you are not satisfied. If, after further discussion, you are still not happy with the situation ask to see the parent governor and the chairman of governors. This should alert the governing body to any disquiet you and other parents may feel concerning the way the school is run and the methods used. You should also put your concerns in writing to the governing body with a request that the matter is dealt with at the next governors' meeting. Once you have gone through all these channels, if you still feel that your concerns are not being addressed, write to or arrange an appointment with your Area Education Officer. Failing a satisfactory outcome, the next step would be to your County Councillor, then to your M.P..

## PARENTAL RIGHTS/ACTIONS

Parents have every right to give an opinion on methods used in schools and if you feel they are failing your child then you have a parental duty to say so. Provided you have a genuine concern and go through the correct channels you should expect your problem to be treated seriously and answers found. If your child is failing to read you need to know the reasons for this and what action the school is prepared to take. If they are not prepared to take any specific action to improve matters you have three courses open to you:
1. Remove the child from the school.
2. Arrange private help.
3. Help the child yourself at home.

## TRANSFER

If you choose to transfer your child to another school, visit first and discuss the problems you have had. As long as the head teacher is prepared to accept him and as long as you can get him there every day, you can send your child to any school, not just the one nearest your home. Bear in mind though that he is likely to fit into the neighbourhood better if he attends the same school as most of the other children.

# PRIVATE TUITION

Should you decide on private tuition it is important to accept that it may take some time to put things right. Choose a tutor who is qualified and very experienced and ask if you can telephone parents of other children who attend. Better still, choose on personal recommendation. Watch for local advertisements but go for one that advertises continuously rather than the odd one-off advert. A reputable tutor will be only too pleased to give you the names and numbers of satisfied customers (with their permission of course) and will always prefer to assess the child personally rather than accept another's opinion. When you take your child for assessment ask for details of qualifications and experience and look for a properly professional attitude and approachable personality.

## HELP FROM PARENTS

The third option is the most difficult - choosing to help your child yourself. It can be done, very successfully, but nobody promises it will be easy. In fact, it can be very, very difficult, not because of the intrinsic problems of the job itself but because of the emotional involvement you have with your own child. It is hard to take a detached view of your children's problems - they matter as much to you as to them, perhaps even more so. However, if it is to work, your attitude must be, "Look! We are in this together. We will crack this together." Then you have to take a gigantic step backwards and try to get an unemotional overview of the situation. Remember that you are the adult. Any tantrums come from the child only. Be calm, be kind, be reassuring. The child desperately wants to please you so show enormous pleasure at the smallest step forward. You can do it and if, as the parent, you can keep cool and remain supportive, at the end of it all you may well have developed a much stronger relationship with your child.

## AFFECTION AND SUPPORT

Painful experiences in learning can detract from the later pleasures of reading. The experience of failure will almost certainly have undermined self-confidence, possibly creating a personality disturbance. It follows, therefore that a non-reader must be treated very delicately. Fear of criticism can be paralysing for a sensitive child. He must be free of undue anxiety in order to make progress. If you are going to help your child to read then you must surround him with affection and support, not carping and criticism. Never punish, ridicule or embarrass. This can cause an aversion to the whole idea of reading, if not to a complete emotional blockage. Children have to be one hundred percent confident in the adult who helps them. They must be in an environment which gives them a sense of security and reassurance, not one which leads to a permanent state of anxiety and the apathy, aggression, fear or hyperactive behaviour which can result.

## PROGRESS AND MISTAKES

Before learning can begin the child must feel that the effort he has to make will be worthwhile, that reading is actually interesting and that some kind of incentive or reward is being offered. He must be reassured that in spite of past failures he can and will succeed. It is essential for him to know that he is making perceptible progress, so keep charts showing how many sight words he knows, how many sounds, how many correct spellings. It is important, too, that he learns to make mistakes and understands that making them is a necessary part of any learning process. Some children will not even try because they are so afraid of being wrong and they must learn that it is better to try and get it wrong than not to try at all. Success is a stimulus to greater effort, failure should be a stimulus to try again. Tell the child that it does not matter if he gets a word wrong. This just reminds you both that he still needs to learn it.

## READING READINESS

Children must be ready to read and a preparation period is vital. The importance of good language development and wide experiences has been discussed in previous chapters. Where these have not taken place it is essential to remedy the situation before starting a reading programme. The child may not have shared a range of experiences with interested adults who can express themselves clearly, who can answer questions and share the excitement and delight. Children need adult company as well as that of their peers and an excellent way of beginning any remedial programme is to arrange exciting visits and experiences in the company of a loved adult based on the child's particular interests. By way of preparation for reading he needs, also, to listen to stories. If having them read to him appears babyish, invest in some talking books and a personal stereo. Opportunities for painting and drawing encourage self expression as do music making and listening. Choosing a pet and learning to look after it is a source of delight and great satisfaction for most children and a comfort and solace for past traumas.

## SELF-RELIANCE AND RESPONSIBILITY

Before they become readers and writers children have to accept the solitary silence of reading as opposed to the social interaction of spoken language, the slowness of writing compared with the speed of speech. They must be able to learn and work on their own and be self motivated, while at the same time being prepared to accept instruction. It follows that the more you give your child responsibility and the opportunity to develop self-reliance, the more likely he is to be in control of his academic development. Children who are used to being cossetted, spoilt and over-indulged may well find it difficult to make the effort to work things out for themselves, to remember word shapes and sounds and put in the necessary hard work to learn to read and write.

## OLDER NON-READERS

Specific difficulties arise with older non-readers. It is no good giving boys of eleven or twelve the same kind of reading materials as seven or eight-year-olds. Although that may be their reading age, their outlook and interests will be those of normal eleven and twelve-year-olds. They will do the same things, like the same things and their reading materials must take this into account. Pay a visit to your local library and ask to be shown the 'easy teens' section. You should find plenty of easy readers there based on the interests of twelve-year-olds and upwards. Explain why you want them and ask if more can be obtained. (I have found librarians particularly helpful in this way and willing to go to considerable trouble to provide a supply of these books.) If you prefer to buy them, enquire at a bookshop and explain the problem. Choose a less busy time and they should be prepared to spend some time with you finding out what is suitable and available. Alternatively you could ask for advice and titles from the remedial department of your local secondary school. Telephone for an appointment and ask specifically to see the head of department. You may find the school prepared to lend you all the materials you require.

## USING ESTABLISHED INTERESTS

Established interests are often a good way into reading and writing, for older children especially. If they like fishing, get books about fishing. If a girl likes riding, find books about horses. The exciting aspect of teaching children individually rather than in groups is that everything can centre on that particular child, his likes and dislikes, his interests and hobbies. Get rid of any school readers that are associated with past failure. Make a fresh beginning with new books, a new approach and a new teacher. These children have already failed with the school's reading methods so do not continue them. Use a new and novel approach. Introduce a different method of reading to avoid the negative effects of past failures and give plenty of opportunities for self-expression and any activities the child likes and can do to raise his self-esteem.

## THE FORMAL APPROACH

Most schools teach reading using the shared reading approach (see Chapter Three) and a great many children fail as a result. I have found that many children who have come to me for remedial help, without exception, have thrived on a more formal approach and I would advise any parents who want to help their children to try this method first. It involves using flash cards to build up initial confidence and enable the child successfully to read the controlled vocabulary readers, then gradually introducing sounds (see Appendix ) and spellings based on the child's choice of words and\or a specific spelling scheme. (I use Schonell.) It involves regular lessons at specific times and work for the pupil to complete between lessons. Nothing is cast in tablets of stone because you are dealing with one individual child and children vary in age, ability and interests. A basic lesson, however, could be on the following lines:

## A BASIC LESSON

1. Four to six new sight words introduced. These would be discussed together, initial sounds pointed out, perhaps put with other known words to make a sentence. Maybe a  game of Snap using two sets of known words.

2 . New sound introduced. (For order see Appendix  Two.) As an example take 'pl'. Say something like, "Look. Here's a p followed by a l. When they are put together we say  the sound pl .Tell me some words that begin with the sound pl." The child might say  play, plums, plate,  plank. Divide into four a page in a plain exercise book, put pl at the top and write one word in each space.

|  pl  |  |
|---|---|
| plate | play |
| plums | plank |

As part of his homework the child has to draw the relevant picture in each space. Next  lesson he is asked to say the sound and read the words.

3. Handwriting (if necessary.) Mainly for younger children.
   Double lined handwriting book.
   One letter per lesson.
   Draw the letter for the child, saying something like:
   "This is letter b. We say its sound b. Start at the top, go down, halfway up and round."
   Together think of some words beginning with b and write them in the book. The child has to complete each line to the end.


b _____

b _____

baby _____

bear _____

bath _____

book _____

banjo _____

4. Creative writing - depending on the age and stage of the pupil.

   For young children:
   "Draw me a picture please." Duly done.
   "Tell me about it." Child does.
   "What would you like me to write underneath? Tell me what to say."
   Adult writes at child's direction. Child writes over or copies later.

   For older pupils:
   A 'conference' on what has been written for homework. (See chapter

on writing for details.) Discussion on how the work could be improved. Encourage suggestions from pupil.

5. Reading:

Controlled vocabulary readers can be obtained from any bookshop. Ladybird, based on the key words is probably the best known but not to everyone's taste. Check that the books have a set vocabulary and are not based on the developmental (or shared reading) approach. Older pupils might read the easy teen readers or books dealing with their own particular interests.

Get the child to read the book aloud to you, encouraging him to use context clues and sounds for new words, though avoid the laborious sounding out of unknown words. (The content of the story is completely spoilt by constant stops and starts and if there are that many new words the book is too difficult anyway.)

Encourage sensible guessing from the context of the story. Actually say, "Make a guess" and give praise liberally. With older readers it is sometimes a good idea to read a page each in turn. Not only does this give the pupil a break, it also provides him with an example to emulate. Be prepared to provide a lot of books. You cannot expect a child to be fired with enthusiasm for reading unless he has a constant supply of exciting reading materials. Show him how much you enjoy them too and make your lessons together rewarding - and fun.

## KEY POINTS FROM CHAPTER 8

1.  Failure to read sets off a cycle of failure which is difficult to break. It can become a personality problem resulting in feelings of discouragement and inferiority.

2.  There is a strong link between backwardness and delinquency. Children try to compensate for low self-esteem by anti-social behaviour, others feign illness. Most are desperately unhappy.

3.  The National Curriculum was supposed to improve literacy. So far it has failed to do so. Although full of good ideas it is not properly implemented because of class size and teacher inadequacy.

4.  A list is given of possible causes for failure to read.

5.  The difficulty of parents judging their children's performance is discussed and suggestions made.

6.  Advice is given on how to make a parental complaint. Options are discussed.

7.  Choosing a reputable tutor.

8.  In order to help their children themselves parents must aim to be calm, kind, detached and unemotional - never easy with your own child.

9.  Because of their previous bad experiences with learning, remedial readers must be treated with great sensitivity and kindness. They must be surrounded with affection, never criticised, ridiculed, punished or embarrassed.

10. The child must feel his efforts are worthwhile and be convinced he will succeed. He must be able to see perceptible progress and learn to accept mistakes.

11. Children must be ready to read if they are to succeed.

12. Specific difficulties with older non-readers are discussed.

13. Use established interests as a way into reading.

14. A formal approach is usually successful where the developmental method has failed.

15. A basic lesson is described.

16. Provide plenty of exciting reading materials. Show your child that you enjoy the lessons too. Make them rewarding and fun.

# 9

# TESTING

## TESTING YOUR OWN CHILD

Testing your own child is not something I generally recommend. Since parents are so emotionally involved with their children it is difficult for them to take a detached view and to see a clear, overall picture of achievement and problems. However, many parents are desperate to get some idea of where their children stand in relation to their peers and, frequently, they do not receive the answers they require from school.

At one time pupils were graded at the end of each term or year and if your young one came eighteenth out of a class of thirty you could feel satisfied that he was holding his own with children of a similar age. This, however, had great disadvantages for the poor child who came thirtieth out of thirty and as child-centred education came into our schools, competition was discouraged and children were expected to improve their own performance without trying to 'beat' their peers. As with many theories of education, this one was carried to ridiculous lengths in some schools, with sports days where everybody 'won' and no idea given to parents as to where their children stood academically in relation to the rest of the class.

Now, with SATS tests at 7, 11, and 14, the pendulum is beginning to swing back but phrases such as "working towards level 2", for example, give the average parent little information. In fact, were you told this of a 7-year-old there might be cause for concern since what it really means is that the child has failed to reach the expected level for that age.

Nor do school reports always give accurate information. "Approaches literacy with enthusiasm" sounds good but might equally apply to a non-reader as to a fluent one. Most parents want scores related to age so that they can tell whether their children are progressing satisfactorily, doing well or falling behind. If you re one of these and do not wish, or cannot afford, to take your child to a private tutor for testing then a case can be made for doing it yourself.

## CHOOSING THE TIME AND PLACE/SETTING THE SCENE

Before you begin any kind of assessment ensure that you and the child are in the right frame of mind. Anxiety on either part can spoil completely any chance of creating a positive and helpful occasion. Always, I tell the child exactly what we are going to do, and why. Whether or not you do the same is your choice. You know your own child and can predict if he is likely to make a scene at the very idea of doing a test with you. In this case it might be better to take a more casual approach, e.g. "Let's see how many of these words you know (or can spell)". However, in my experience, children see through subterfuge very quickly and I prefer to be completely honest with them, saying something like: "I want to find out how well you can read. This is called a reading test and it will tell us your reading age."

Choose a time when you can remain completely uninterrupted for at least an hour. Send out the rest of the family, disconnect the telephone, remove the pets, do whatever it takes to ensure complete privacy and quiet.

The place should be comfortable, with no visible distractions.(For this reason the child's own room or a playroom, for example, is not ideal.) Sitting at the kitchen or dining room table is suitable. Have ready to hand paper, pencils and the tests you intend to use.

## BEGINNING THE TESTS

Normally, I begin with a non-verbal intelligence test which involves just drawing on the child's part. It is fairly relaxing so tends to dispel anxiety. With the Goodenough-Harris Drawing Test the child is given a plain A4 sheet of paper and asked to draw the best possible picture of a man, big enough to fill the page. A mental age is obtained from the score, gained by allocating marks according to the list given. If the mental age is equal to or above the child's chronological age, then attainment should be around the same level. However, if his mental age is way below his actual age, he cannot be expected to be reading at the same level as most pupils in his school year.

Gaining an idea of inherent ability is an important first step in assessing attainment because attainment should match *ability* rather than *age*. Unfortunately, the author has been unable to obtain permission to reprint the test here (it can be found in the Aston Index, published by LDA) but even without establishing a mental age it is possible to assess where a child stands in reading and spelling in relation to his actual age.

## READING TESTS

Some children begin reading by recognising the shapes of whole words, some guess according to context, some use phonics to work out new words. Accordingly, two reading tests are given, a sentence test, where context is useful, and an individual word tests based on word recognition or 'sounding out'. Encourage the child to read as far as he can.

## THE HOLBORN READING SCALE *

\* Every effort has been made to establish ownership of this test which is believed to have been published in 1948 by George C Harrap and Co. Anyone laying claim to its copyright is requested to contact the publisher.

The Holborn Reading Scale, which follows, is administered thus:
The child is asked to read the numbered sentences and stopped when he makes four mistakes in the same sentence. The age at the end of this sentence is his reading age. No help should be given. When mistakes are made, make no comment or correction, just let him continue until the fourth mistake is made in the same sentence, then stop the test.

1. The dog got wet and Tom had to rub him dry                               509

2. He was a very good boy to give you some of his sweets.          600

3.  My sister likes me to open my book and read to her.  603

4   Go away and hide behind that door where we found you just now.  609

5   .Please don't let anyone spoil these nice fresh flowers.  606

6.  The string had eight knots in it which I had to untie.  700

7.  Wine is made from the juice of grapes which grow in warm countries.  703

8.  Mary went to the grocer's to buy some sugar and some syrup  . 706

9.  Quench your thirst by drinking a glass of our sparkling ginger ale.  709

10.  The people could scarcely obtain enough food to remain healthy.  800

11.  Elizabeth had her hair thoroughly combed and her fringe cut.  803

12.  By stretching up, George just managed to touch the garage ceiling.  806

13.  Father had a brief telephone conversation with my cousin Philip.  809

14.  This coupon entitles you to a specimen piece of our delicious toffee.  900

15.  The chemist could not suggest a satisfactory remedy for my headache.  903

16.  Nobody recognised Roger in his disguise as a police official.  906

17.  Leonard was engaged by the Irish Linen Association to act
    as their London agent.  909

18.  Judged by his photographs your nephew is certainly a
    peculiar character.  1000

19.  The examiner was impatient when I hesitated over a
    difficult phrase in my reading.  1003

20. Delicate individuals should gradually be accustomed to gentle physical exercise.     1006

21. The musician whose violin was interfered with has our sincere sympathy.     1009

22. The soloist was not in a convenient position for seeing everyone in his audience.     1100

23. Christopher omitted to acknowledge the receipt of Michael's annual subscription.     1103

24. The secretary said there had been a substantial increase in the Society's expenditure.     1106

25. The Borough Council decided to celebrate the occasion by organising a gigantic sports festival .     1109

26. It is essential that engineering apprentices should acquire some good technical qualification.     1200

27. Particulars of the careers of eminent men will be found in any good encyclopedia or biographical dictionary.     1203

28. Certificates of insurance will be issued to all policy-holders paying the necessary premium.     1206

29. The ceremony ended, appropriately enough, with the Choir and Orchestra joining in the National Anthem.     1209

30. It is both a newspaper which chronicles events and a magazine with the usual miscellaneous features.     1300

31. The necessity for accelerating the work of the Economic Conference was repeatedly emphasized.     1303

32. These documents constitute an authoritative record of a     1306

unique colonial enterprise.

33. Psychology is a science which seems to fascinate both the adult
and the adolescent student.                                        1309

Scores at the end of each sentence are given in years and months. Thus 1309 means 13 years 9 months. Similarly 800 means 8 years.

## THE SCHONELL GRADED WORD READING TEST*

* The Schonell Graded Word Reading Test, from the Psychology and Teaching of Reading by Fred J Schonell, is reproduced here by kind permission of Addison Wesley Longman.

This is based on individual words which may be recognised as whole words or sounded out. Again, no help is allowed but give lots of positive encouragement and praise. Show the child that the words must be read across the page, starting at the first one, explaining that they are separate words and will not make a sentence. Point out that the words get harder as they go on but the first ones are quite easy. Encourage the child to read as far as he can until he has failed on ten successive words. Then give him an opportunity to look at the remaining words to see if he knows any of them. If so they can be added to his score. The words must be absolutely correct to count, with the stress properly placed e.g. can<u>a</u>ry not <u>canary</u>, <u>pos</u>tage, not pos<u>tage</u>. Neither correct the pronunciation nor say any word the child gets wrong.

See Test Overleaf.

## The Schonell Graded Word Reading Test

| | | | | |
|---|---|---|---|---|
| tree | little | milk | egg | book |
| school | sit | frog | playing | bun |

| | | | | |
|---|---|---|---|---|
| flower | road | clock | train | light |
| picture | think | summer | people | something |

| | | | | |
|---|---|---|---|---|
| dream | downstairs | biscuit | shepherd | thirsty |
| crowd | sandwich | beginning | postage | island |

| | | | | |
|---|---|---|---|---|
| saucer | angel | ceiling | appeared | gnome |
| canary | attractive | imagine | nephew | gradually |

| | | | | |
|---|---|---|---|---|
| smoulder | applaud | disposal | nourished | diseased |
| university | orchestra | knowledge | audience | situated |

| | | | | |
|---|---|---|---|---|
| physics | campaign | choir | intercede | fascinate |
| forfeit | siege | recent | plausible | prophecy |
| colonel | soloist | systematic | slovenly | classification |
| genuine | institution | pivot | conscience | heroic |

| | | | | |
|---|---|---|---|---|
| pneumonia | preliminary | antique | susceptible | enigma |
| oblivion | scintillate | satirical | sabre | beguile |

| | | | | |
|---|---|---|---|---|
| terrestrial | belligerent | adamant | sepulchre | statistics |
| miscellaneous | procrastinate | tyrannical | evangelical | grotesque |

| | | | | |
|---|---|---|---|---|
| ineradicable | judicature | preferential | homonym | fictitious |
| rescind | metamorphosis | somnambulist | bibliography | idiosyncracy |

Scoring should be done as unobtrusively as possible but carefully and systematically on a separate piece of paper. Keep the scoring sheet on the side furthest from the child. If you are right handed sit him on your left, if you are left handed reverse this. The actual counting of the score be done later in the child's absence. Schonell's suggested method of marking is thus:

Make a dot for each word read correctly, a small cross for each wrong word. If you keep to the pattern of the test you can refer to it later for diagnostic purposes. The score sheet for a 9-year-old might look something like this:

```
.  .  .  .  .
.  .  .  .  .
.  .  .  .  x
.  .  .  .  .
.  .  x  x  x
.  .  .  x  x
x  x  x  x  x
x  x  x        test stops here.
```

Total correct words: 24

Having obtained the child's score his reading age is derived from the following norms (revised 1971) *See overleaf.*

| No of words Read correctly | R.A Yrs. Mths | No of words read correctly | R.A Yrs. Mths |
|---|---|---|---|
| 0-1 | 6.0 minus | 46 | 9.3 |
| 2 | 6.0 | 47 | 9.4 |
| 3 | 6.2 | 48 | 9.5 |
| 4 | 6.4 | 49-50 | 9.6 |
| 5 | 6.5 | 51 | 9.7 |
| 6 | 6.6 | 52 | 9.8 |
| 7-8 | 6.7 | 53 | 9.9 |
| 9 | 6.8 | 54 | 9.10 |
| 10 | 6.9 | 55 | 9.11 |
| 11-12 | 6.10 | 56 | 10.0 |
| 13-14 | 6.11 | 57-58 | 10.1 |
| 15 | 7.0 | 59 | 10.2 |
| 16 | 7.1 | 60 | 10.3 |
| 17-18 | 7.2 | 61 | 10.4 |
| 19 | 7.3 | 62 | 10.5 |
| 20-21 | 7.4 | 63 | 10.6 |
| 22-23 | 7.5 | 64 | 10.7 |
| 24 | 7.6 | 65 | 10.8 |
| 25-26 | 7.7 | 66 | 10.9 |
| 27 | 7.8 | 67 | 10.10 |
| 28 | 7.9 | 68 | 11.0 |
| 29 | 7.10 | 69 | 11.1 |
| 30 | 8.0 | 70 | 11.2 |
| 31 | 8.1 | 71 | 11.3 |
| 32 | 8.2 | 72 | 11.4 |
| 33 | 8.3 | 73 | 11.5 |
| 34 | 8.4 | 74 | 11.6 |
| 35 | 8.5 | 75 | 11.7 |
| 36-37 | 8.6 | 76 | 11.8 |
| 38 | 8.7 | 77 | 11.9 |
| 39 | 8.8 | 78 | 11.10 |
| 40 | 8.9 | 79 | 12.0 |
| 41 | 8.10 | 80 | 12.1 |
| 42 | 8.11 | 81 | 12.2 |
| 43 | 9.0 | 82 | 12.3 |
| 44 | 9.1 | 83+ | 12.4 |
| 45 | 9.2 | | 12.5 |
| | | | 12.6 |
| | | | 12.6+ |

In the case quoted, the score of 24 would give a reading age of 7 years 6 months, well below the child's chronological age.

# SCHONELL SPELLING TEST*

From this the child's spelling age is calculated. Each word from the test is said aloud by the adult, first as a single word, then in a sentence, then on its own again. At this point the child is asked to write down the word, e.g. "See. I can see you. See. Now write the word `see'."

The words must be taken in the order given, reading across the page. When ten consecutive words are incorrect stop the test.

| | | | | |
|---|---|---|---|---|
| see | cut | mat | in | ran |
| bag | ten | hat | dad | bed |
| | | | | |
| leg | dot | pen | yet | hay |
| good | till | be | with | from |
| | | | | |
| time | call | help | week | pie |
| boat | mind | sooner | year | dream |
| | | | | |
| sight | mouth | large | might | brought |
| mistake | pair | while | skate | stayed |
| | | | | |
| yolk | island | nerve | join | fare |
| iron | health | direct | calm | headache |
| | | | | |
| final | circus | increase | slippery | lodge |
| style | bargain | copies | guest | policy |
| | | | | |
| view | library | cushion | safety | patient |
| account | earliest | institution | similar | generous |
| | | | | |
| orchestra | equally | individual | merely | enthusiastic |
| appreciate | familiar | source | immediate | breathe |
| | | | | |
| permanent | sufficient | broach | customary | especially |
| materially | cemetery | leisure | accredited | fraternally |
| | | | | |
| subterranean | apparatus | portmanteau | politician | miscellaneous |
| mortgage | equipped | exaggerate | amateur | committee |

The Schonell Spelling Test from The Psychology and Teaching of Reading by Fred J Schonell is reproduced here by kind permission of Addison Wesley Longman

Mark the test afterwards and find the spelling age using the formula:

$$S.A.= \frac{\text{no. of words correctly spelt}}{10} +5$$

so if a child spelt 35 words correctly his spelling age would be 8.5 years or 8y. 6m. (Decimal years are translated into years and months in the following way: .1=1m. .2=2m. .3=4m. .4=5m. .5=6m. .6=7m. .7=8m. .8=10m. .9=11m.)

## TESTING PHONICS

Begin by asking the child to say the alphabet, then explain that letters have sounds as well as names and that you are going to find how many of these he knows. Start on the bottom line and point in turn to each letter, asking the child to say the sound it makes when it begins a word( e.g. `a' as in apple, `b' as in book - but note that x says its name). If he says the sound correctly colour its box with a highlighter, so that the letter still shows through.

Then move up to the blends and explain that two letter sounds can be run together to form a sound blend. As before, go along each line of blends, highlighting those known.

Climb the tree to the silent `e' words and check if the child knows the rule about silent `e' making the preceding vowel say its name. Continue up the tree, highlighting as before, to the vowel and consonant digraphs, explaining that two letters can be put together to make a new sound (not run together as with a blend).

Final consonant blends come at the ends of words. Ask for examples of these as well as checking the actual sounds. With silent letters the child needs to know which letters come after these silent ones and to give some examples here, too e.g. silent `k' is followed by `n' as in `knee'. The section on endings requires examples, also.

Stop the test when the child fails to get any sounds correct in a section but give him the opportunity to look over the remaining ones in case he can pick out the odd one here and there. At the end of the test you will have a clearly marked picture of his phonic knowledge and teaching can begin from here.

# THE PHONIC TREE

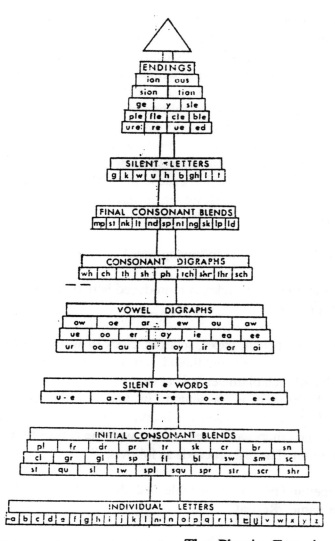

The Phonic Tree is reproduced here by kind permission of the University of Reading.

## MIXED LATERALITY

Sometimes, children who experience reading and writing difficulties are found to have mixed laterality. Normally , in right-handed people, the left hemisphere of the brain is dominant; in left-handers, usually the right hemisphere is the dominant one. Occasionally, however, inconsistent laterality causes a child to be, for example, left-handed but with a right dominant eye or ambidextrous with a left dominant eye. There can be various combinations of mixed laterality and in my own experience, over many years of teaching, I have found over and over again that children with initial reading difficulties (almost always boys) display mixed laterality. Why this is so is not entirely clear but the effects appear to lessen as they get older, possibly because their brains gradually adapt to this less usual configuration. However, it may explain early problems in acquiring literacy.

Laterality can be tested in the following way;*

* This test, from the Aston Index is reproduced here by the kind
  permission of LDA.

Materials required: pencil, paper, scissors, clock or watch, football, small ball, a pack of cards, needle and thread, screw-lid jar, toilet roll tube,sheet of paper with half inch diameter hole at centre.
Each part of the test is presented, in turn, to the child and the hand/ear/eye/foot which is used is observed and noted. Apart from the kick-ball test, the others can be carried out with the child sitting at a table opposite the tester. The test proceeds as follows:
1. Write
   Place paper and pencil on the table. Ask the child to pick thèm up and write his name. Repeat.
2. Cut
   Place paper and scissors in front of the child. Ask him to cut out a square. Repeat.

3. Throw ball

Put a small ball on the table. Ask the child to throw it, with one hand, to the tester. Repeat.

4. Thread needle

Put needle and thread in a central position and ask the child to pick it up and put the thread through the needle. Repeat.

5. Screw lid

Place the screw-top jar in front of the child and ask him to remove the lid. Then take these from him and place them one on the other in a central position on the table. Ask him to screw the lid on again. Note the hand used. Repeat.

6. Deal cards

Note the hand used for placing individual cards on the table. Ask the child to deal seven cards to each person. Repeat.

7. Telescope

Put the cardboard tube on the table. Ask the child to look through it at a particular object. Note which eye is used. Replace the tube on the table and ask him to look through it again, this time at a different object. Repeat.

8. Binocular test

Note the eye used for looking through the hole. Ask the child to hold the piece of paper with the hole in at arms length, with both hands. The tester then holds up a pencil and asks him to look through the hole at the pencil, then slowly bring the paper to his eye, looking at the pencil all the time. Repeat the process with a different object.

9. Kick ball (preferably done outside!)

Place the ball a few paces in front of the child. Ask him to take a short run and kick the ball. Note which foot is used to kick. Repeat.

10 Ear

Place a watch or small clock on the table and ask the child if he can hear it ticking. Note which ear is put to it. Turn it over and ask him if it is louder or softer that way round.

Scoring

The object is to note any inconsistencies in laterality. A maximum of 10 points is given for all items being unilateral (all right or all left). 2

points are taken off this maximum for each item performed on the opposite side to the most frequent response. So if a child performs 8 tests right and 2 left his score would be 6. A low score indicates an individual with poor lateral dominance. Commonly, in my own practice, I have pupils who are generally left-sided but have a right dominant eye and ear and for some reason, little understood, this appears to create initial problems with reading and writing.

## LEFT/RIGHT AWARENESS

There is some evidence that poor readers are weak in left/right awareness. To test this sit the child opposite the tester and ask him to show his left hand. Then hold out both hands and ask, "Which is my right hand?" After this, ask the child to point to his own right ear, then touch the tester's right hand with his own left hand. It soon becomes obvious if he has difficulty in differentiating between left and right.

## DYSLEXIA - see appendix 5

In conclusion, it is always better to have a child assessed by a professional. However, if you do decide to test your own child, try to prevent it becoming a fraught occasion. Be encouraging, not critical, supportive, not carping. Reassurance and praise are an essential part of any testing, even more so when the tester is the parent.

Children should be valued for what they *are*, not for what they can *do* but every child has the right to receive help to overcome any problems in developing literacy.

# CONCLUSION

In these days of rapid technological change, of sparkling visual images, vicarious experiences and a world seen across our television screens, the question arises, why read? Children can get all the information they need from television - so goes the argument. Certainly they are extraordinarily responsive to visual imagery. Even the rowdiest class falls silent the moment the television tube flickers into life. Even very small children remain riveted to the screen for considerable periods. Children learn easily and enjoyably from television. Many toddlers know scores of songs and rhymes, not learnt at their mother's knee but at the television screen. It is a tremendous vehicle for learning and has an instant appeal for almost every child in the land - and most adults too.

Previously information came from books and those who had access to it were in a position of social superiority. Now much information is available visually but those who can search for it, process it and evaluate it have the advantage. Although the technological revolution is gathering pace we are not yet at the stage of talking to our computers. Written and read words are still the vehicle for requesting and receiving most information, even when via the computer. Indeed, it could be argued that an ability to read and write is a distinct advantage when it comes to handling and processing the masses of information and entertainment available to us. Society is going through tremendous change and no-one can be sure how things will develop. The social trend of 'cocooning' however is growing and, were it to continue, instead of going out to work and socialise people would shut themselves in, working, talking and socialising through computer networks. Children might not attend school but do their lessons on line. All this is based on words written (or keyed in) and read. In order to take most advantage of it people would have to be not only computer literate but word and language literate also. Illiteracy would become even more of a handicap.

When society goes through periods of rapid change people begin to cling to old values for fear of losing them. It is certainly true to say that there is more interest in children learning to read and write now than there has been for many years and it has become a more prominent issue. So many things depend upon it. Complicated instructions for video recorders and microwaves have to be read and understood, drivers have to be able to read traffic signs and traffic notices, even couch potatoes who sit in front of the television all day need to read which programmes are on when. In fact there are arguments to say that literacy is more important now than it has ever been and not only for its usefulness. Television has opened a world of literature to many who were not previously aware of it and wonderful stories watched on the screen can inspire the public to read more. It can be no coincidence that most of the best selling books are related to television series and films.

Accepting the vital importance of literacy, it is essential that every parent ensures that their own child is developing normally in reading and writing. They cannot depend on the school to alert them when a child is falling behind. Schools are at the mercy of the latest educational theories and though many have been tried the search still goes on for the perfect teaching method. Schools are overworked and understaffed and, if the latest HMI report is to be believed, thirty percent of all lessons are unsatisfactory. No modern society has achieved the goal of universal literacy. There are always some children who fail and it is up to individual parents to ensure that their children are not among them.

# APPENDIX ONE

## FORMATION OF LETTERS

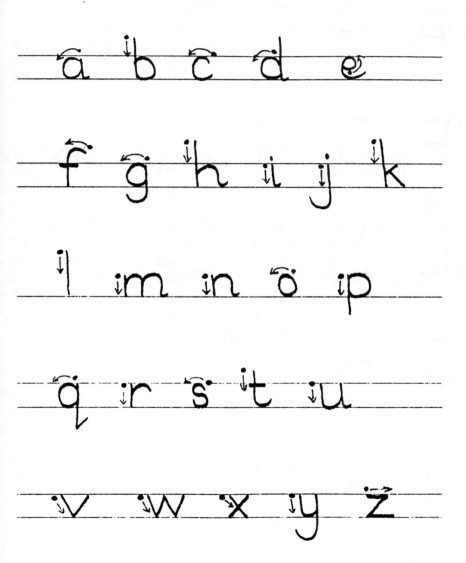

# APPENDIX TWO

## SUGGESTED PHONICS PROGRAMME

**Stage One:  individual letter sounds.**

a b c d e f g h i j k l m n o p q r s t u v w x y z

**Stage Two:  initial consonant blends.**

bl br cl cr dr fl fr gl gr pl pr qu sc sk sl sm sn sp st sw tr tw scr shr spl spr squ str

**Stage Three:  silent e**

a-e  e-e  i-e  o-e  u-e

**Stage Four:  vowel digraphs.**

ai ar au aw ay ea ee er ew ie ir oa oe oi oo or ou ow oy ue ur

**Stage  Five:  consonant digraphs.**

ch pc sh th wh sch shr tch

## Stage Six:  final consonant blends.

ld lp lt mp nd ng nk nt sk sp st

## Stage Seven:  silent letters.

b g gh h k l t u w

## Stage Eight:  endings.

-ble  -cle  -ed  -fle  -ge  -ion  -lion  -ous  -ple  -re  -sion  -tion  -ue  -ure  -y

## APPENDIX THREE

## MOST COMMONLY USED
## WORDS

**One quarter of all reading is said to contain these words:**

a and he I in is it of that the to was

**With the following, one third of all reading:**

all as at be but are for had have him his not on one said so they
we with you

**With the following, one half of all reading:**

about an back been before big by call came can come could did
do down first from get go has her here if like into just little look
made make more me much must my no new now off old only or
our other out over right see she some their them then there this
two up want well went were what when where which who will
your

As a result of their research for the Ladybird Key Words Reading Scheme,
Ladybird produced a list of three hundred key words - those most
commonly occurring in children's and adult's reading. These were
published as a Key Words Card and may still be available from:

Ladybird Books Ltd.
Loughborough
Leicestershire.

These key words were used in the early books of their reading scheme.

## APPENDIX FOUR

## WORD PATTERNS AND
## RULES

In the English language most rules seem to get broken. Nevertheless, it is worth teaching the regular rules and patterns to which the majority of words will conform.

for example:
a vowel, followed by a consonant then a silent e, means that the vowel says its name, not its sound. Thus:
tub  tube
man  mane

certain other letters are regularly silent:
k followed by n is silent, as in
knee
knight
w followed by r is silent, as in
wrist
writing

When a word ends in f, in its plural form the f is removed and ves added.
wolf  wolves
shelf  shelves

Words ending with y preceded by a consonant lose the y in plural form and add ies
puppy  puppies
baby  babies

These are just some examples of the rules and patterns which should be taught to a structured plan. There are various books available. Ladybird publish The Ladybird Book of Spelling and Grammar which is a useful addition to their Key Words scheme. One book I would strongly recommend is from

Ward Lock Educational Company Ltd.
1 Christopher Road
East Grinstead
Sussex  RH19 3BT

Called `The Old Fashioned Rules of Spelling Book', it is very clear and straightforward and is in the form of a workbook.
ISBN 0-7062-4085-5

**APPENDIX FIVE**

**DYSLEXIA**

The word dyslexia comes from the Greek

dys - difficulty
lexis - words

and accurately describes the condition - difficulty with words. It may pertain to the spoken word but, more often, occurs with written language, affecting both reading and writing. No-one really understands its cause, although it is known to be constitutional in origin and, often, an inherited condition. Basically it means that a dyslexic child will have more than usual difficulty in learning to read and write, often referred to as a specific learning difficulty. In pre-school years, it may manifest itself in late development of language, difficulty in repeating patterns and sequencies and fitting things together (e.g. jigsaw puzzles), clumsiness and uncertainty as to being right or left handed. The British Dyslexia Association believes ten percent of all children to have some degree of dyslexia, with four percent severely affected. This means that in a school of two hundred pupils, eight children could be severely dyslexic.

The condition cannot be prevented, nor cured, but a great deal can be done to alleviate its effects. The major problem is one of identification. By no means all children with reading difficulties are dyslexic but many do have the condition and need special help with very structured programmes which take into account the peculiarities of dyslexia, for example, that what appears to be known today may be completely forgotten tomorrow.

There are specific tests which can be given to any child who may have the condition (the Bangor Dyslexia Test is one of these) and if you strongly suspect your child suffers from this contact:

The British Dyslexia Assosiation
98, London Road
Reading
RG1 5AU

There are many signs which point to dyslexia:-
- confusion between left and right,
- difficulty in fastening buttons, shoes etc.
- particularly messy work,
- words spelt differently each time they are used,
- poor handwriting
- difficulty in following a set of instructions,
- difficulty in learning to tell the time,
  and so on.

The British Dyslexia Association produce a detailed list of indications, available from them at the above address.